CHASE BUTTICE

Witchy Bitch

A Revolution in Reclaiming Your Self-Worth and Divine Feminine Power

I dedicate this book to all the sensitive ones. You are the wayshowers of this new world. May this book help guide you back to remembering the depths of your spiritual power.

Contents

Introduction

Witchy. Bitch. How do these words make you feel? Ashamed, Empowered, Dope, Angry? They are definitely two words that even to this day can stir up the soul of any woman. So why the hell would I choose to make the title of my book something that most people shun? Because it is now, for the first time in thousands of years, that we Witches can come out of the closet. This book is for them.

This Witch doesn't wear a black coned hat and rides around on a broomstick (although this is still my favorite costume for Halloween); it's the everyday Witch. It's for the stay-at-home mom who follows her intuition to drive her daughter to school that day, only to find out the school bus has an accident on the highway. It's for the HR executive that has a hunch not to hire this one guy despite his impressive resume and then learns he has been known to sexually harass his coworkers. It's for all the people who don't even know they are Witches. It is for everyone. The truth is that **a Witch is an empathic, healing, intuitive person that is guided by love**, simple as that. She is the Everyday Witch. She isn't this elaborate and enigmatic mistress of the night who has all kinds of creepy tools and casts spells to lure men into her bed. No, she is the single female on a Friday night eating a pint of ice cream and watching a cheesy-ass romantic comedy (*guilty*)—yeah, that's her too.

The Everyday Witch, surprisingly enough, can be male or female, but there has been a special sect of society (cough, *religion*) that has carved out the Witch as explicitly female and explicitly evil as she represents all the dark powerful aspects of the feminine, i.e the power of intuition, psychic awareness, and subtle energies. Because of this, we have all but completely lost these god-given natural powers as we have been taught to fear them at all costs. But they still remain, lodged in the dark crevices of our subconscious. This book is to help you remember them, reignite them and guide you back to your true nature, and ultimately your divine power.

Returning to Balance

The word Witch is locked up in layers of cultural turmoil that can still cause a hush in a crowd. There is a darkness that surrounds it, especially for anyone that grew up religious. This is a distortion of a deep, loving power that got lost in the shadows. The aim of this book is to reclaim this word and identity, bring it back into the light, and remember what its original power was. Because a real Witch is someone that holds and channels the energy of the Divine Feminine at its highest degree. Traditionally, Witches were the wise women of a community. They were the known healers. They mended broken bones, broke debilitating childhood fevers, and delivered babies to terrified new mothers. They were good; they were love. They were so connected to the natural world that they were at one with its rhythms and cycles. They were in tune with the deeper, subtle energy that runs our everyday material reality, and acknowledged that energy as a very real thing. They were the seers—those channels that had access to the Spirit world—and could dispense messages from other realms to assist and heal. These women had a mysterious hidden power and worked in the hidden realms, realms they didn't fully understand or need to understand but were simply a part of. Women are literally the portals of all life on this planet; the most magical and mysterious of all earthly truths, birth. Think about that for a second. No human being would exist on this planet if it wasn't nurtured, carried, and cared for by a woman's body. There is an innate connection that cannot be denied in this power. And it is time this magic be remembered, revered, and cherished.

The Monotheistic religions of the world have created a great imbalance of power between the energies of the masculine and feminine on this planet. The feminine had no place within these dogmatic and rigid structures and was therefore deemed "Witchcraft" and the work of Satan. Because all the major monotheistic religions have been male-dominated, a deep fear of this feminine power developed. The inability to "understand" or "control" these subtle energies added to this fear and a widespread campaign to eradicate this "power" went underway. What is funny is that this has happened throughout all of human history, in all three prominent monotheistic religions. To compensate for this scorched spirituality, each religion at some point developed their own "mystical" sect that opened to the deeper mystery of God and integrated magic. Unfortunately, those sects live on the fringes even to this day. The feminine eradication conditioning runs *deep* and has been refining itself for thousands of years now inside of every sect of our culture and ourselves. Even to this day in the 21st century, the word Witch is used as a pejorative all over the world. All of us have been trained to *fear* our own intuition, our own inner voice, and the deep knowing we hold within. We have been trained to fear ourselves, and only trust outside sources as the word of truth. This to me is the precise reason we are so lost on planet earth today. We have all forgotten the deep well of connection within.

Let's make no mistake, this universal feminine energy also exists in men. Every human being, every living being on this earth for that matter, has a balance of these forces within them. Humans, specifically, have just been deeply conditioned to deny this magic and only rely on the "rational" faculties. We are now at a time in human history that we can begin to *safely* open to the feminine without fear of being exiled for it. All of us—male and female, straight, gay, asexual, queer, trans, all of it—ALL of us have been labeled and placed in a category that distorts our light in some way. Because of the rigidity of thought throughout the religious orders of the world, there has been very little room for that which resides *outside* of the system. We have all therefore been shaped into something that doesn't quite fit our raw, authentic, magnificent essence that is original and unique, never to be replicated. We are at a time in history where the suppression of the feminine has reached its tipping point. Mother Earth and her peoples are no longer willing to suppress this well of power, emotion, and magic any longer.

The Patriarchal World Culture or PWC (this term coined by the genius of Regena Thomashauer who wrote the seminal book, *Pussy$_1$*) has a one size fits all approach to life; and it is based on duality, hierarchy, and control. You are either this or that, black or white, right or wrong, and if you aren't, you don't fit *in* and are therefore "bad." All of humanity has suffered under this system as it has squashed our individual essence.

It also robs us of the truth that no-thing and no one is simply one thing. Nature is made out of paradox; two things co-existing at once, and both being true. The Taoists understood this four thousand years ago in China as the simple and ancient symbol of the yin/yang encompasses this truth. The yin and the yang are not two separate beings, one male, one female, with all the energies that represents. Instead, the yin and the yang are one. They are opposites that exist simultaneously and rely on one another to express themselves fully. The yang cannot live without the yin and vice-versa.

In Taoism, health and well-being are dependent on the balance of these two energies. If one is more dominant than the other, then dis-ease results. Our entire natural world, and universe for that matter, is made up of this principle as we see it all around and within us. We have active times and resting times, we have daytime and nighttime, we have socialization and solitude, etc. The list goes on and on, but what is important to note here is that we need a balance of all of these energies to be fully healthy, in tune, and at our highest level of consciousness. We need this balance of opposites, the tension it creates and the dynamic power that results from them both co-existing simultaneously to allow for our essence to shine through.

If either of these energies are out of balance, we will begin to feel the effects of dis-harmony and dis-ease. It is clear everywhere. For instance, someone constantly doing, doing, doing with no rest will eventually get sick or get anxiety that will force them to stay down and rest. The body and the natural world regulate pretty well. It is normal for these energies to shift and move from one side to the other, as they are dynamic forces constantly in flow. The issue we have today is that the scales have been out of balance for a very long time. They have been stuck, and stagnant. There has been no movement, no shifting of power or dynamics. We have been masculine dominant for thousands of years now and Mother Earth and her peoples feel it deep in their bones. We are parched, and we crave the deep intuitive waters of the feminine. We are all beginning to instinctually recalibrate this force inside and outside of ourselves. The difference between today versus our past is that so many souls are waking up to this deep imbalance that we can freely recalibrate this energy without fear of persecution or suppression. That doesn't mean that there won't be forces that will fight this new shift in consciousness, but now for the first time in many, many years, there are more of us than them. The scales are shifting and the old masculine dominant world is fading.

True health (ours and the planets) is a complete balance of these masculine and feminine energies, the yin and the yang. We need the knowing, emotion, and quiet of the feminine to remind us of the mystical nature of reality. It employs the feeling realm, where our empathy and sensitivity live, connecting us all to one another. The feminine is about "being," while the masculine is about "doing." And we need both energies holistically dependent on one another to function at our highest.

This is true for men, too, as the imbalanced male/female energy means they, too, must fit into a very narrow scope of masculinity that robs them of their own intuition, sensitivity, and empathy. The deep imbalance means the men have had to carry the burden of a system that robs women of their power but simultaneously gives ALL of the power to them when they may not even want that burden or responsibility. So when I discuss the PWC, please understand I am bringing light to a system in which ALL of us have suffered.

To heal, the scales of energy must be rebalanced, not just simply "power." The feminine energy of the world must rise, and the masculine energy must wane. Men, if in tune with the Divine Masculine, will feel this as a giant weight being taken off their shoulders as they are allowed to explore the more mystical, intuitive aspects of their nature (something traditionally they have never been allowed to do). At the same time, women will begin to embody a deeper sense of integrity and worth, beginning to own and command energy on this planet that is more sensitive, empathic, and alive. Let's not fool ourselves here, there are plenty of women on the planet that carry the attributes of the masculine- in other words they themselves are masculine dominant. Most women and HUMANS I meet tend to be masculine dominant as this is how we have been taught to compete and truly survive, at least in the USA. This is also the reason the world is in such peril at the moment, our systems are breaking, and so many of us are so sick. Feminine energy is an energy- its a way of being, and it's time that it rise, in ALL of us.

This is why I wrote this book. In my private practice, the consistent theme I saw with all of my clients was that they had no grounded spiritual practice. Sure, they understood the power of meditation and mindfulness, but did they understand what it meant to really pray and connect to their soul? No. They had maybe read a lot of self help books and understood things rationally but deep in their bones, they had no idea how to integrate this truth. They didn't understand what true faith in something deeper meant and were not able to fully trust their own deep inner knowing. They were committed to their rationality while all the while knowing that something deeper gnawed at them. This "something" was their own deep intuitive connection to the spirit world. The disconnection between most women and this source of power is a great fracture in our psyche's and souls, because this is the natural expression of the feminine- its deep knowing, its deep psychic undercurrent, and it's deep emotional well. These are all hidden aspects in our society that are never given credence to or taken seriously. But they are real, and bringing them to the surface, naming them, and beginning to work with them and connect them to your daily life will bring about a complete revolution in the self.

The thing we have forgotten in this era is to value our intuitive connection to the spirit/unseen world. This should be the central priority of our being, our own personal and individual connection to God/The Universe should be the *most* important and central theme of our life. It is, after all, the essence of our being intermingled with its origin. All of us have a different way of connecting with the etheric. Some hate the word God, some love it, some prefer Universe, others simply like LOVE. For me, I resonate with 'Spirit' so I will be using that for the most part throughout this guide.

Once we have an established connection to this force and are grounded within the self, the masculine/rational/doing faculties can then assist the feminine in finding its way on the material plane. The doing should always be informed by the being, not the other way around. The way we live now, the world is operating from a "doing" place- where "should" resides. What ends up happening is we use our brains, and egos to move forward in life versus our own deep knowing. We ignore our own inner well and get caught up in the drama and the storms created by others. The "shoulds" of our reality then begin to guide our actions versus our own higher self and deep connection to the mystery. The mystery then begins to fade as we perpetually ignore its presence.

Because becoming healthier both individually and collectively means more focus, sitting with and cultivating the energy of the feminine. Think of this as a manual to reclaim your Divine Feminine nature and reclaiming the healing Everyday Witch from within. You are taking the time to prioritize your own deep inner knowing, recalibrating the self and therefore the planet. Because you are choosing to place focus and intention here, you are actively enhancing your self-worth. As that rises, all other forgotten pieces of yourself will come back to you. We are reigniting our deep feminine wisdom and dismantling the deeply entrenched conditioning that all of us have undergone that has prevented us from fully owning and claiming our own authentic energy and power on this planet. It is a journey to remembering your deep, divinely given connection to Spirit and beginning to own that connection while bringing conscious awareness to the damaging internalized rhetoric of our mainstream culture. The Earth depends on us, simple as that. She is ready to embrace the feminine and the feminine is ready to be seen.

Divided into 6 chapters with questions, practices, and spiritual guidance from my own life and healing practice, this book will take you on a journey very deeply into yourself so that you can begin to live a life that is authentically your own. One that is in command of your own energy and power, remembering your honor, integrity, and self-worth. Please use this book any way that suits you. You can gobble it up in one fell swoop or slowly integrate it over time. There are journal prompts at the end of each chapter to help you dig into your subconscious even deeper, unveiling truths, and finding your voice. My main request is that you use this book, actually use it, put it into practice. Don't simply read it and shelf it- get into it, get dirty, speak to God out loud, find out what is really inside of you, ignite your own inner flame and remember deep well of feminine wisdom that lives inside of you.

WITCHY BITCH WISDOM

- The truth is that a Witch is an empathic, healing, intuitive person that is guided by love, simple as that, the Everyday Witch.
- All of us have been trained to fear our own intuition, our own inner voice, and the deep knowing we hold within. We have been trained to fear ourselves, and only trust outside sources as the word of truth. This is the precise reason we are so lost on planet earth today.
- To heal, the scales of energy must be rebalanced, not just simply 'power'. The feminine energy of the world must rise, and the masculine energy must wane.
- The thing we have forgotten is to value our intuitive connection to the spirit/unseen world. The central priority of fully conscious beings is our own personal and individual connection to God/The Universe. This is the most important and central theme of our life.
- *Doing* should always be informed by the *being*, not the other way around. The way we live now, the world is operating from a 'doing' place- where 'should' resides. What ends up happening is we use our brains and egos to move forward in life versus our own deep knowing.
- Now is the time to reignite our deep feminine wisdom and dismantle the deeply entrenched conditioning that we have

undergone that has prevented us from fully owning and claiming our authentic energy and power.

Endnotes

1. Regena Thomashauer, *Pussy.* (Carlsbad: Hay House, 2018)

1

Feeling Blessed, Protected, and Guided: Making Space for the Sacred

"The human race is a very, very magical race. We have a magic power of witches and wizards. We're here on this earth to unravel the mystery of this planet. The planet is asking for it."
~Yoko Ono

The first step in reclaiming your worth and power as the sovereign being you are, is to establish a connection with Spirit. This is the most important piece of anything I will explain to you in this book. From this connection, the wellspring of magic that lives within you may emerge. Without it, our inner and outer world are empty, devoid of meaning, and mechanistic in many ways. Connecting to this source of love may sound easy enough, but it is something that is felt deep within rather than intellectually. It takes focus and true emotion; it takes real truth. **That is essentially what this entire book will help you do; get back into your body, and most importantly your gut-**

where your intuition resides.

Most of us live in a box of "shoulds." The shoulds can come from anywhere, through any means. God knows us empaths wish to please the closest people to us. We want to make sure those around us, whether it be friends or family, are happy, and we feel on a deep subconscious level that we "should" do things in order to keep harmony. We may not even be conscious that we are living by this edict, we simply feel this gnawing feeling of "needing" to do a long list of things-mostly to keep others in our life happy. The shoulds we live by are self-imposed and paradoxically dictated by the culture around us. Yet because we abide by them, we perpetuate them.

The thing about the shoulds is that they decide the direction of our lives. And because they almost always come from outside of ourselves, not from within, at some point we feel we are living someone else's life, and not our own.

So in this first week, we'll explore how to tap the realm of Spirit, where our higher guidance lives. That which guides us from within. Intuition can only work through our feelings and through bodily sensations. When you tap into your truth and power, gut and instinct, you'll become more aligned with the truth of who you are.

Our feelings are the feminine realm, where our true Witch power resides.

Most of us live in our heads and completely out of our bodies. This is because, traditionally, religion demonized the body, especially the body of the female. We have been conditioned to feel shame about our bodies since birth-yet another sub-conscious way the mystic powers of this universe have been subdued. What better way to disconnect the feminine from itself than to teach it to hate itself? The advent of Newtonian science liberated us from the cage of religion. In turn it placed us in a larger cage- one that made us "seem" free but completely cut us off from the energetic realm of Spirit. This time, we were "free" to make up our own mind, but not if it included anything mystical or unexplainable. Science needs "proof" of the miracle of nature. It removed the scornful God that was placed upon so many of us, yet in turn, with the same energy, then disregarded the awe and miracle of our world. In one fell swoop it eliminated the realm of magic cutting us off from the unseen and the mystery of life. Anything that couldn't be explained rationally was then disregarded in this paradigm and with it so much magic died. The didactic nature of what our reality has become—atoms and molecules—has turned so many of us into machines. Machines don't feel; they do.

Reclaiming our Divine intuitive nature as the sacred feminine vessels on this planet reinstates *feeling* back into our world. We are all desperate to feel more, yet often this is seen as being weak, a "pussy," etc. We have been taught from a very young age to just suck it in, swallow it down, and move on. It's what our culture tells us makes us strong and keeps us competitive. **This is essentially internalized patriarchy—a constant need to know, compete, and be first. In truth, it only perpetuates judgment of each other and keeps us doubting ourselves and our self-worth. This constant competition keeps us with our eyes on each other instead of within.** We forget our own deep connection to a higher source that when accessed and felt, can transcend any "competitive" environment with miracles of its own making. It is also what keeps us in the box of "shoulds."

I don't know about you, but being born a sensitive, empathic

3

woman in such a masculinized culture made me grow up to feel incredibly worthless. That is because based on the dominant paradigm, there was literally no "worth" in what I had to offer the world. I have always been incredibly intuitive. I could just sense things about people and, from a very young age and was frequently asked, "How do you know that?" The answer was always the same, "I don't know, I just do." Paired with psychic dreams and occasional visions, as I got older, I just became more and more of an outsider. There wasn't anywhere within my culture I could look for help, mentorship, or assistance with this power. No one mentioned that it was a powerful, real gift; it wasn't even discussed! Mainly, it just made me weird. My mom and I would joke about being Witches from time to time as she has a very powerful intuition. Yet this power is kept deep underground, in the shadows of her subconscious, as she herself has been never fully awake to her abilities. It's as if she knows that she has them, but they are so innate to her that she is not fully aware of them or how to wield them.

In high school, I would go to the occasional tarot card reader but never felt like the people I saw were truly genuine or could even sense what I could sense. I was always searching for a mentor or teacher, but they were almost all but destroyed. I was always naturally drawn to the archetype of the Witch; it was always something with which I resonated. Think about it; it is one of the only female archetypes of our time that has magical powers (let's just forget that little bitty part where she is deemed "evil.") Magic was always something I knew was real, and I was drawn to those that believed in it, although it was always hidden away in the dark corners of Wicca and Paganism. I remember watching *The Craft* as a young teenager, do y'all remember that movie? It quickly became my favorite movie as I

4

watched it over and over. The women had supernatural powers and were real Witches, come on! But yet again, I was confronted with the cultural stereotype of a Witch: someone that used their magical powers to manipulate and bend material reality to their will. Someone who messed with the natural order of things and was essentially evil.

I was confused by all this dark witchcraft because I knew I was actually really good. I have always been good; I was born good. I have wanted nothing, since I was born, other than to help, heal, assist, and love my fellow humans, yet I had nothing to name my power against. I didn't dare call myself a Witch at a young age; Witches were evil, and I wasn't. But it was consistently the only energy I resonated with in terms of what I carried within me.

I was born a very sensitive, intuitive, and empathic woman; in simple terms, I was born a Witch. The flip side of this power was that I was so empathetic that I felt almost debilitated by my sensitivity. I over-ate from a very young age to quell the pain I felt for the world which perpetuated an already deflated sense of self. Being bullied horribly in junior high didn't help any of that either and, by the time I got to high school, I was nearly 300 lbs and severely depressed.

It took me years to find my path and even give myself the time and space to acknowledge my gifts. And that is just it, these gifts I was born with— the gift of deep empathy and intuitive sight, of being able to work with energy, and of naturally navigating the realms of the unseen, were never seen as anything worthwhile. These energies have been thrown deep into the realm of our cultural shadow, as we have been so embedded in the rational for so long, we have forgotten the sacred realm of Spirit.

I know many of you reading this book haven't really had a

real connected spiritual practice, maybe, your whole life. You may not have had any crazy psychic experiences. But I can bet that you are highly empathic, which makes you extraordinarily powerful as empathy is the gateway to intuition. What I found in my private practice is that most of my clients were at a breaking point; they felt empty and exhausted, unable to find their authentic truth or access who they really were due to living their entire lives out of "shoulds." I would listen to and try to assist them through the rational context within which they were operating which was never able to truly get to the root of the issue, or begin to shift their vibration. It was like fighting fire with fire.

The most profound quote I have ever heard is by the great Albert Einstein, he said that "You cannot solve a problem from the same level of consciousness at which it was created." I think about this all of the time and use it to inform all of my work. Albert Einstein himself was a Witch, using imagination and dreamwork to conjure his theory of relativity. He understood the other realms of consciousness and integrated them into his work.

"You cannot solve a problem from the same level of consciousness at which it was created." - Albert Einstein

Continuously trying to solve your problems from the same level of consciousness they were created is like beating your head against a wall, and it is where so much of humanity dwells. We must go deeper to access real truth and alchemize it. That is why I believe what we're all so desperate for—on a primordial and visceral level—is a connection to Spirit. We crave the release of control and to begin to *allow* the unseen magical energy of the universe to flow through us and direct us instead of our flawed human selves trying to run the show (which ultimately becomes incredibly exhausting).

Over and over, clients would come in to see me when I was doing bodywork. I would listen to and eventually ask them the question that, by then, I knew would truly put them on the required track to transforming their lives the way they so desperately wanted. That question was, "Do you have any kind of spiritual practice?" Almost always, I got the same answer, "Not really," "Kind of," and "I try." Many described feeling empty and yearning to know themselves deeper yet had no real connection to Spirit. This is because we have nothing in our culture that is outside of any religious or philosophical dogma that gives us an option! The funny thing is, **when you begin to connect with Spirit on a daily basis, you remember who you truly are and discover the depths of your own spiritual power, which is what is so desperately needed for people on this earth today.** No one ever teaches us about the unseen realms and how to connect to them in a non-religious way– or how to fully own and command our own connection to Spirit. Yeah, there is the genre of "new-age" that has been helpful in my life, but still, nothing gave me the real sense of empowerment and deep connection that I was seeking. Nothing ever taught me how to fully own and command my own power as the divine female I was, Spirit incarnate, and a Queen in her own right, just as you are.

Contemporary society validates meditation, and yes, meditating calms my mind and chills me out *sometimes*- but the truth is that I always yearned for more. And, when I was younger, meditating was a kind of psychic torture in some ways as I was so wound up from being in the world of "doing" that trying to sit quietly and observe my thoughts made me feel nuts. I know that the way out is to begin to observe yourself, but at that time, it just made me want to crawl out of my skin. Meditation aims to empty our minds of thoughts and become present with the now. It wasn't enough. I wanted to be filled up with the Divine, to communicate with God in a very real way.

The problem was that I had no context or way of knowing how to do that outside religion. So, I stayed in the dark. I spent many years searching other cultures, attending medicine ceremonies, and exploring every facet of spiritual life on the planet. But it wasn't until I came across the work of Tosha Silver and Florence Scovel Shinn that I finally got permission to create my own spiritual life communing with the vast expanse of Love. I was desperate for the sacred, and finally, **when I opened up to it and subsequently created a practice around it that was made** *from me* **and no one else— designed and orchestrated by my** *rhythm* **and no one else's—that** *came from my soul* **and nobody else—and that was when my entire life changed.**

The funny thing is that when you begin to connect with Spirit daily, something begins to happen inside of your soul, you begin to remember who you truly are. When you commune with the invisible, it's like you open a kind of portal to another world. And in that world resides the deepest, most authentic part of yourself, a part that was lost along the way. Even in the "new-age" world, there is very little material on teaching one how to pray or connect to the unseen realms in a non-religious way.

And that is precisely the purpose of this book. Think of it as permission to cultivate your own living, breathing relationship with this force. There is no dogma or concrete beliefs. No, this spiritual practice is innately embedded in the energy of the Divine Feminine. It is based on feeling, love, and healing, and it is collective instead of hierarchical. This is reclaiming your own Queen-Goddess-Priestess-Witch power, and, my God, is it the way out of living in a constant state of fear.

Journal Prompts

- Did you grow up in a spiritual tradition? If yes, how has that shaped your spiritual practice today? If not, what, if anything, has replaced it?
- How does cultivating a prayer practice actually make you feel? Nervous? Stupid? Excited?
- When you think of a higher power, what images or ideas come to mind? How does this influence the quality of your connection?

Opening Up to the Flow

To become more in tune with your Everyday Witch power, acknowledging and opening up to the flow is imperative. So, right now, I am calling this force "the flow," but I often call it Spirit, too, among other names. You are free to call it whatever the heck you want. It is the universal life force energy that emanates and animates every living thing in this universe.

We cannot deny that there is an energy behind all the matter in this world, an energy running through us that shapes our world and the universe. This energy is the same all throughout the cosmos; it is what moves galaxies in a spiral formation, just as it makes the grass grow and our hearts beat. It is a pulsing, spiraling energy that simply IS. We see it in the way hurricanes form and how our toilets flush. This energy is within us and IS the universe. We are it, it moves through us just as it

9

is us. You can call this energy whatever you want; Universal Life Force Energy, Chi, Spirit, Prana, Source, God, Love, the Divine. There are innumerable names to try and name the ineffable, but for our little human brains to use and commune with this force, it is helpful to name it. Naming it will help you begin communicating with this force so that it may guide, protect, and bless you. I want you to think about what word feels most comfortable for you. It doesn't matter what it is; it's all about what *feels* right.

You may feel that you've been so steeped in rational energy your whole life that all you know is that something is missing but have no idea how to actually access your *true* feelings. This, too, is okay. Having enough conscious awareness to tune in with yourself to know that something feels off, and choosing to read this book, means you are ready for this journey. Just beware, it will feel pretty uncertain, unstable, and plainly put, kind of weird. But that is because you are remembering a forgotten paradigm and energy– one that has resided within you all this time, that has been dormant. This energy is ready to awaken but be patient with it and yourself; it may take some time and fumbling around in the dark. So that's what we're doing here: putting words, power, and feeling to these forces of love. I promise you that if you stay on this path, you will get there. The entire reason that we need to begin to name this force is so we can begin to *feel* it. Because when we *feel* it, it actually becomes real to us. And that is what I want to get across here; what we are doing is putting words, power, and feeling to these forces of love. This is a real universal living, breathing energy that we all have access to. When we begin to engage with it on a real level, we start to feel it all around us and within us.

When we name this force—the universal energy we all have access to—we can begin to *feel* it. And when we *feel* it, it actually becomes real to us.

Throughout my practice in working with people on a spiritual level, I have come to understand that what keeps us ensnared in situations, conditions, jobs, relationships, etc., is fear. And um, yeah, that shit is real. We are trained to be afraid from the moment of leaving the womb. And this was one of the reasons I always kind of envied religious people because, in a way, they had a one-up on me. It's like they were in this special club with a direct link to God. It's like God was gonna hear and listen to them because they were a signed-up member, and I wasn't. Not having that "official" connection just contributed to my already insecure being.

When we feel connected to this force of love that is the Divine —but also so much more, we begin to trust in all of life more. We're able to relax. The advent of modern science is incredible and has connected us far more than at any other time in human history, but fundamentally it is fear-based, or doubt-based which is just another word for fear. There is already enough of that in the world—just turn on the news or read your social media feed. Cultivating your connection to Spirit and the Divine Feminine offers a way out of this maze of uncertainty. It is opening our consciousness up to the idea that there is actually a force out there and in here that is good.

Women, in particular, grow up bound by centuries of psychic abuse and trespassing. I see this time and time again in my private practice. Women describe the same problems in their bodies that their mothers and grandmothers had. This stored-up inter-generational trauma keeps us locked up, afraid and

11

tense. This is a real thing, y'all. We are all connected on this planet—whether or not we feel it—our consciousness is shared. The imbalance of feminine power and the trespass of the sacred feminine energy have made us *all* pretty tense.

I woke up to this just in the past couple of years as I realized that I always have a low level of tension throughout my body. I always seemed to be on alert; it was as if fear was keeping me safe. The responsibility was on *me* to keep myself safe, which was a lot of pressure. These days I know that Spirit has my back and is always guiding, protecting, and blessing me, allowing me to breathe a little. When I first introduced the sacred into my life, it was like I was unclenching muscles that had been held tight my whole life. And because I was unclenching, I noticed how much more relaxed I felt, also how sore I was from the tension!

Journal Prompts

- Do you "feel" a connection to something greater than yourself?
- Do you believe in a force greater than yourself? If so, are you ready to cultivate and commune with it? How does that idea make you feel?

Creating Your Altar Space

This is essentially where it all begins, y'all—the altar. You can look up what an altar looks like on Pinterest or Instagram if you have never seen one, but essentially it's a space dedicated to your spiritual practice. The altar is the first step in actually creating a literal and figurative space for yourself in your life that is singularly dedicated to your inner voice, intuition, and connection to a force that is greater than yourself.

What I would continuously see in my practice, were women that felt lost and uncertain of themselves and their truth while simultaneously having no literal space in their lives where they sat and connected with Spirit. It kind of makes sense, how can you find your truth if you don't give yourself time to access it? All of us have a deep inner truth that is constantly giving us signs and cues, it is Spirit working through us. But because we are so indoctrinated in this culture to go, go, go and do, do, do, we are running all around all the time drowning out this inner voice that is ever so gently guiding us.

Crafting the altar is way beyond self care. This is your power seat, your throne. This is where the magic happens because you are consciously choosing to make room in your life to give back to yourself in a way you never have before. Women and most empaths have been trained since birth to give. Because the masculine/yang energies have been much more valued, women/yin have been trained for millennia to serve that energy. What eventually happened through this process was that women actually gained their sense of self-worth through the act of giving. Which meant that to receive actually made one feel kind of shameful, as if that woman wasn't doing her job right. Her job was to give so if she were to receive it would mean she wasn't worthy. This is why women specifically, and for so long, have had such difficulties feeling worthy, because we were literally trained since birth that giving is where our sense of self worth came from.

This toxic over-giving pattern is one of the biggest challenges in overcoming constantly feeling depleted and exhausted. This practice of sitting at your altar means that you are finally choosing to give back to yourself. You are choosing your own life, and essentially you are deciding that it is time that you access the deep well of power that lies dormant within you begging to be tapped and expressed.

So, if you constantly feel depleted and exhausted, examine your beliefs about giving because it is a toxic pattern to over-come. This practice of sitting at your altar means that you are finally choosing to give back to yourself. You are choosing your own life, and essentially you are deciding that it is time to access the deep well of power that lies dormant within you, begging to be tapped and expressed.

The first step in creating an altar is to clear a space in your house that you can fit a cushion positioned on the floor in front of a small table or shelf set against the wall If sitting on the floor hurts your body, sit in a chair and adjust the table height to the appropriate level so you can comfortably gaze at the special items you will place on your altar. This means that you need to consciously pick and clear a space along a wall that is large enough for your body and your table that you will adorn with beautiful, symbolic objects. It's fine if the best you can do is create a private corner in a room where you can be alone at times. This act in and of itself, clearing an actual space dedicated to yourself and your spiritual practice is monumental. This is revolutionary and I commend you for taking this step, it's big. What will eventually happen is that we will begin to internalize this altar. Once we learn how to pray, connect, and express our souls truth, we can begin to carry that around with us. What ends up happening is that we can access this altar space internally, wherever we go, and at any time. Secondly, I'm going to ask you to find a candle to place on the table that is no higher than your chest height while sitting down. These are the basic elements to creating an altar; a table, cushion, and candle. From here, the rest is all about YOU. The rest is all colored by your own flavor, color, and individuality. There is no universal symbol or doctrine I'm asking you to follow, the only thing I'm asking you to do is think about what energies you want to bring to your altar. Because this is your power seat and sacred spiritual seat, I want you to think about the kinds of images, words, artwork that makes you feel empowered and awake. You are remembering who you and more importantly who you want to become. If you're not sure where to start, I'll share some examples of who I have at my altar and why.

In building an altar, you remember who you are and, more importantly, who you want to become. I have four "power images" I like to call them, on my altar, and I switch them out if I feel called to or if something new strikes my fancy that I want to bring in. You don't need to have 4 images, one will do. I simply felt four was right for me. The first image is Isis, goddess of magic and wisdom in Egyptian mythology. I can't explain why I love Isis, I just do. And for the things that I place on my altar, I don't have to explain anything to anyone. I remember when I lived in Seattle, someone had written on a very busy street wall, "Isis is a goddess not a terrorist." That was probably to this day one of the most profound pieces of "graffiti" I've ever seen. When I saw that written, it hit me so deeply how far we have come from worshiping the divine feminine, her name + magic- to instead worshiping death, under the same name. It's time ISIS came back, in her true form. To bring the waters of healing, rejuvenation, and high priestess seeing energy back to the earth as she originally did. So she is there, she helps me remember who I am at my core. And she is connected to *The*

15

High Priestess archetype of the Tarot which is part of my own destiny.

The second image is of the Mayan Moon Goddess, Ixchel. I'm not Mayan, but my good friend was. She is an herbalist and a very strong and powerful woman, a Witch—although she would never dare call herself that. I think people had demeaned and put her down her whole life for her intuitive seeing. But I saw who she was. She was magical. She helped me after a difficult time in a medicine ceremony and told me to pray to Ixchel for protection. I found an image online that struck me deeply. It's black and white, a side profile of Ixchel sitting on her legs, back straight, head held high. The image gives me a deep sense of power and integrity; it imbues me with that energy as I look at it. Ixchel is holding a flower and petting a rabbit and has a snake on her head and feathers coming out of her hair. She is fierce, and I find her very comforting and powerful. She teaches me how to have integrity and hold myself like a fucking Goddess.

The third image is from a dream that felt very significant. As I started doing more profound work on myself, "shadow inquiry," as I like to call it, which we'll explore later in the book, I started getting into deeper and deeper layers of my subconscious. One night I had a dream of a black jaguar. She was walking along with a deep grace and knowing, this great cat held a deep primordial power and wisdom. She held magic inside of her and deep seeing of truth. I remember feeling fear, moving back into the bushes to hide. When I woke up, I sat with that dream throughout the day and had the realization that the jaguar was, in fact, me. It was my shadow, the part of me where all of my power lies, the part I am afraid of. That is what that image reminds me of every day. To not be afraid to go deeper and bring light to the parts of me I am afraid of.

16

When we face our deepest fears and our own darkness, we discover our deepest power.

The fourth power image is a charcoal drawing of a horse my friend drew. This image also was related to a dream where I was riding a beautiful horse through green hills. I was galloping and felt so free and wild. I realized that as I began to feel afraid of how fast we were going, the horse would absorb the fear and slow down. In the dream, I realized that I was slowing myself down with my own fear. I was able to let it go and allow myself to gallop as fast as I desired; it was exhilarating and empowering—the definition of a *wild dream*. When I woke up, I realized my dream was a metaphor for life and how energy literally works. There is a deep universal benevolent flow, and if we open ourselves up to it, it will just carry us, and we can ride it wildly. But because of our conditioning to be fearful, we slow it down through our resistance. This image reminds me to **let go and just ride.**

So those are my four power images. They are all connected to significant events in my life and remind me of where I am heading, who I want to be, and who I am. This is what I would recommend to you, too. Maybe sit and journal about significant events, people, and animals that have affected you and shifted your perspective somehow. These are energies that you feel inspired by and that resonate with you on a deep level. Things you are naturally drawn toward that represent healing, love, and power. They could be images from a significant dream, or ideas that you are continually drawn to for reasons you cannot fully understand. In our new practice, we actively embrace the unknown as part of the 'mystery'. We do not demand to know why—we simply accept and allow.

I'd also recommend studying some of the different Goddesses of different cultures to see if any resonate with you. You can look into your own ethnic heritage and deep roots and find the feminine archetypes of that lineage. It is so empowering to begin to dig into your roots and find the lost feminine inside of it. Another option is to ask yourself, "Who is a Goddess to me now?" Who inspires the heck out of you? And is it someone you look up to? That is who should be at your altar.

The other objects that make my space specific to me and like my own little sanctuary, are crystals. If you aren't into crystals, you don't have to go out and get any. This is just what I resonate with, as they carry an energy that somehow elevates my spirit, again I don't really understand how or why, I just simply accept it. I have some labradorite and a few different kinds of quartz and amethyst. If you are interested in crystals, I encourage you to visit a crystal store or go online and just allow yourself to be drawn toward the ones you really like. There will be something in you that resonates, and you don't even have to explain why you love it. You just do, which means it is serving some part of you.

I also have some crow feathers on my altar. I used to live in the Pacific Northwest, where these birds flock in huge numbers, and I used to collect feathers on long walks with my dog. Over time I collected so many feathers that I have a kind of bouquet at my altar that makes it really beautiful. I call this my "crow medicine" and feel connected with this beautiful, intelligent, and sacred bird. Birds play with and defy gravity, they are transcendent creatures, and I like to honor them and bring that energy into my altar space.

I always have some palo santo on my altar. This tree grows in Brazil and when the wood is burned slowly it gives off the most delicious aroma; sweet and sacred. You may prefer sage or cedar as it is earthy and cleansing or incense. The whole point of burning things (besides, it's cool to burn stuff and watch the smoke) is to cleanse the energy of a space. It's just a nice thing to do when you sit at your altar after lighting a candle- to light some palo santo and cleanse your energetic area. It creates a ritual for yourself and makes what you're doing feel sacred and important. And this is exactly what a Witchy Bitch is, a sacred and important embodiment of the Divine Feminine itself.

And this is exactly what a Witchy Bitch is, a sacred and important embodiment of the Divine Feminine itself.

By setting aside a space and creating your altar, you are beginning to honor the Divine Feminine in your own way, on your own time, and as you like. By doing this work, collectively, we are honoring *ourselves*, our energy, our being, and beginning to claim our energetic space on this planet. These exercises increase our power, and help us venerate, bow, and align with our own deep primordial, feminine power that has been hidden and held underground for way too long. So now it is time to give yourself space by creating an environment that is sacred, beautiful, and safe to connect and align with the highest energies of this universe.

Think about what objects are sacred to you and collect them all in a sacred space that IS your altar space. This is your power seat and the root of where all of your spiritual power will grow. Treat yourself like a damn Priestess because YOU ARE ONE!! This is your personal art project, and it's all about whatever makes you feel good. This is all based on healing, love, worthiness, and empowerment. Use those energies to create a sacred space in which you feel nestled inside. you feel.

Journal Prompts

- Do you have an idea of where your altar is going to be?
- Who inspires the heck out of you? Who do you find yourself gravitating toward as a leader/role model time and time again? What makes them so special? What unique characteristics do they have? Do you see parts of yourself in them? What parts of yourself do you wish to grow to be more like them?
- Do you have a family member that you were close to that passed away? Do you have a picture of them? Why were they so special to you? What was the unique connection you had to them? How did they make you feel?

Opening Prayer

Once you have your altar set up as you like it, think about how you want to begin to commune with Spirit. What I found doing this Witchy Bitch program with my clients is that many of them felt really awkward and were kind of fumbling around when asked to pray. They had never prayed in their life, or they had prayed in a way that was based within a religious context that was laid out for them in an ancient written script that carried no true depth of feeling and was simply going through the motions. What I realized would be helpful to my clients was to create an opening prayer that established the initial connection to Spirit that was created from their souls.

Now here we are getting into some Witchy shit y'all. An opening prayer begins to use your authority, voice, and power to connect with the unseen realms of Spirit. It is the initial verbiage that you feel comfortable saying to initiate this connection. All of this is in the deepest vein of healing and love.

When I first started dedicating myself to my spiritual practice, I would sit down, light my candle and palo santo, and say this opening prayer: "I pray to the highest source of Love that emanates and animates every living thing in this universe. I pray to love itself." As I was just beginning this work as well, I didn't really know how to pray either, but I wanted to establish the connection by acknowledging this force and inviting it into my consciousness.

When you are developing your opening prayer, ask yourself:

1. What is it that I want to say to this source of Love?
2. How do I want to address it?
3. What will make me feel I am establishing a true connection to it, letting it know I acknowledge it and allowing it to acknowledge me?
4. How do I want to feel when I'm saying these things?

Another opening prayer could be, "I open myself to connect with the highest realms of love and healing." Or something like, "I now allow myself to open to your Divine power and healing love and acknowledge this energy as sacred and powerful." There are tons of opening prayers you could come up with. The most important thing is opening yourself to create something powerful and meaningful to *you*. Something that makes you feel like a true Queen who is worthy, powerful, and connected to the highest realms of the Divine to serve love.

As I said, this is all designed by and for you to get in touch

21

with YOUR personal, powerful flow, to initiate your sovereign and individual connection to Spirit as the Queen-Goddess-Witch that you are. Beginning to own this energy and honoring the Goddesses that have come before us, holding this power and this energy is part of receiving and initiating our own worthiness. It is through this process that we begin to realize our own worth and power as the sacred healing vessels on this planet. Establishing this connection is the foundation of everything that will come after this and is the core of becoming a true Witchy Bitch.

Praying

Actually, beginning to pray, meaning that you are speaking out loud to this force of Love that you acknowledge and bow to, is the first piece of communing with Spirit. When we pray, we open up our most vulnerable self. Praying is so intimate and liberating. When you start to believe and trust and cultivate this force of love in your life, you'll realize that you can begin to expose yourself to it so it may assist you in true transformation. This is why I believe prayer is so damn powerful.

Saying the things that have been haunting you aloud to a loving force and asking for assistance with those things is truly one of the most powerful things any human can do to open up to true transformation.

Praying is powerful for a few reasons. Firstly, because no one is around and it is really just you and God. You are the most vulnerable you could ever truly be, ever. This means you get real with what is going on with you and open yourself up in a way you never could—even with a best friend, family member, or shrink. Secondly, you are beginning to externalize and offer your pain and suffering (whatever it may be) *back* to Spirit.

You are asking for help and freeing yourself from carrying the burden alone. This initiates an incredible alchemical process. Thirdly, by giving your pain over to the Divine, you create a witness for your deepest shadow and darkness. This validates and heals by this simple act alone.

How long have we spent in agony over the silent things that haunt us and that we can't really discuss with anyone else? Exposing yourself to Spirit gets you to the root of it all, so you can truly be honest with yourself. It's the deepest, most authentic, and profound kind of shadow work that can ever be done when spoken with humility and in the name of love.

What is interesting about this work is that there is incredible validation and a true alchemy when we expose our deepest fears and darkness to anyone or anything. When we say it out loud to a friend, it brings it out and up— when we say it out loud to a family member who can see us, we are validated and seen. This is the powerful concept of having a Witness. The difference here is that when we say it out loud to Spirit, we externalize things that we may not even have realized were bothering us because we don't have any kind of human judgment reflecting all our own issues and triggers back at us. It simply goes out into the ether, freeing us.

Having Spirit as our witness gives us a chance to actually process all of our own fear and pain out loud. It's literally like taking a gigantic weight off our shoulders. Exposing ourselves to this source of Love is a pure act, and it is where the deepest work can really begin to occur.

When I first started praying, I would begin with my opening prayer and then sit quietly to open myself to the universe and to allow my consciousness to become one with it. Then I would just start to talk, and for some reason, this would usually be in the nighttime when I could access my own darkness the best; it felt most private and sacred. I would just simply start talking, allowing myself to share with this benevolent force everything I was really afraid of. And usually, it always would come down to fears, but these were deep hidden and long denied that I had never fully acknowledged. When I opened myself up in this way and began to explicate my pain in such an intimate and authentic way, I would discover things I didn't even know existed that were going on within me. It's like I was able to access my truth, where so much shame and unworthiness resided because I was giving my darkness literally back to love. And this is one of the very important core pieces of becoming a true Witchy Bitch, living and residing in *truth* as a foundational aspect of your being.

Truth is imperative when we pray because we are being witnessed by Spirit. We live in an age of denial, which has gotten humanity to where we are all at now. The denial is the numbness of our emotions and the darkening of our clarity, where we "pretend" to keep everyone and everything in its place. It's where everything is "okay." We stay in a state of denial because it is how the world has been run for millennia. Most of us were never in an environment where speaking the truth or sharing our truth was well received or even acknowledged. The denial has been the thing that has kept us safe. The thing is that humans are waking up now, and the consciousness on planet earth has become too bright. We cannot continue the denial patterns of our past in good conscience. It is up to every single one of us, individually to come to terms with our own denial. We must become familiar with where we dismiss ourselves and our truth time and time again because this is the center of our own unworthiness. And this is the center of much darkness on the planet.

Truth is the cornerstone of prayer, as it is beginning to unearth the denials we have kept within us that have kept us living a life that is not our own.

The Cornerstone of Prayer: Truth

So what does your truth mean? It means giving yourself permission to speak the thing you have long denied, a truth you have kept covered and hidden to "fit in" or make others more comfortable.

When we start being more truthful with ourselves, we develop a deeper sense of integrity as we *allow* ourselves to acknowledge the things that are not working for us and maybe never have. This may be the first time that you have ever been this honest with yourself. Truth is the first step in remembering who you truly are; it hollows you out. The darkness or unacknowledged aspects of the self keeps our consciousness limited and hindered. It's like a cloud blocking the sun. It's very hard to access your true authentic power when you're not being truthful with yourself. Opening and exposing that denial clears away the hazy dark mist that keeps us asleep to ourselves and the world, locked in a maze of anxiety, fear, and worthlessness. Beginning to access the truth of ourselves creates true clarity and brilliance. It connects us with our power because we operate from the deepest essence of our being unimpeded by layers of uncertainty. The truth of ourselves is also where our pain, as well as our gifts, reside. When we open to our shame, we open to our power; they are two sides of the same coin. Embracing your truth, no matter how painful, is the true mark of a spiritual warrior and Witchy Bitch. And I say this with complete and total honesty; it *really* does set you free.

We are essentially bringing love and light to our deepest fears- our shadow and the part of ourselves we have no desire to identify with. We are exposing our own darkness, those things that plague us and beat our hearts and minds up senseless. Those things we can't seem to let go of. The power of speaking with intention, vulnerability, and humility to Love itself is a sacred core of Witch power that was somehow lost to us. There is soooo much relief in prayer. But again, it's on *your* terms, in your way, and what feels right for you. I'm simply giving you permission and guidelines to explore all of this. There is so much power in prayer. And as you begin to own your healing power and take up space as the sacred Divine intuitive vessel you are—Mother Earth and Spirit incarnate—you will begin to be able to harness this power for the good of all on this planet.

Journal Prompts

- Have you ever prayed? If so, what was that experience like for you? Did you simply recite scripture, or were you able to access your deeper feeling self and find a kind of communion with the Cosmic Flow?
- Try and develop an opening prayer for yourself at your altar every time you go to sit down. What is something you can say that feels empowered and stretches you a little but isn't completely out of your comfort zone? You can use my original prayer to start and add or subtract from that, or you can come up with a completely original opening prayer.
- How does praying make you feel now? Awkward? Happy? Released? Do you feel comfortable or strange?
- What would it take to feel more power, clarity, and connec-

tion to a force greater than yourself? Can you begin to own this power?

The Realm of Spirit

All of this work is beginning to open yourself up to the unseen realms of Spirit that exist in the energetic realm, the realm beyond matter. This is the feminine realm, the realm of yin, that which is in the ether beyond what our worldly material brain can actually fathom. It's where the feeling realm resides, it's where we sense things. It is also the realm of dreamtime and where we get messages that are not of the rational linear paradigm. As we begin to open and acknowledge this unseen realm that resides through-in and through-out us, we can also begin to open ourselves to acknowledging the presence and power of those that have been in our lives and have past in the physical and begin to ask them to directly assist us in evolving, transforming, and uncovering the truth of who we are. Now, this may sound kind of woo-woo, but nobody knows what the heck happens when we die, except maybe Anita Moorjani, who wrote an entire book on it called *Dying to Be Me*₁ that I highly recommend. She experienced the other side as one of complete love, unity, and magnificence. Still, none of us *really* know because we are all still alive. Even people who have had near-death experiences only went so far and came back.

My dad died in 2015 after years of battling heart disease, stroke, and chronic health problems. Throughout my life, I've had dreams of some deceased relatives or strange visitations from ghosts that felt like they were coming from other realms. Still, I never had real experiences connecting with Spirits on the other side on a consistent basis or truly believing that there were beings along the way guiding me. This all changed after my Dad died. He was a magnanimous being, a full-blooded Italian, wild, crazy, and hysterically funny who had spent thirty years in the record business. They called him the "Bulldog" because he rocked that world—discovering, signing, and promoting some of the best music that has come out of American rock history. He toured with Queen, the Eagles, the Cars, and the list goes on. He wasn't the best father—which I have done quite a bit of work around and healed—but man was he dynamic. My point here is that he lived his life very LOUDLY. And I mean literally. He always had music blaring at the max wherever we would go in the car, music and vibration was constantly around. I came to realize that this translated into the spirit realm seamlessly. Our essence is our essence and is never taken away, even when the body is lost.

After my dad died, I was completely broken by grief while incredibly present inside of the natural world. I missed my dad, we had a very rocky relationship, but toward the end when he could barely talk or do much, we became close. I missed him, and I started to talk to him just here and there to feel connected. As I began to do this, I started getting slapped in the face with direct messages from him. At first, I had a hard time believing it because they were so literal, but little by little, because I was so vulnerable and missed him so much, I allowed myself to believe these messages were really him. *I allowed myself to believe in magic.* My dad opened the gate for me to learn how to connect with higher guidance, guidance from the non-physical realm, which led me to this very space writing these words to you today.

I remember maybe two months after my dad died, I was a total and complete wreck. I had just moved from Alaska to Seattle to be near my sister after breaking off a four-year relationship.

I felt so depleted and exhausted from this relationship and was battling the worst depression of my life, struggling to function. Talk about all the things that were secure in my life vanishing–I was experiencing death in so many forms all around me; material, physical– it was too much for my system to compute. Grief overtook my entire being and I had problems functioning out in the world.

My family had helped me get an apartment and all the stress of moving, trying to find a place to live and feeling uncertain about my path had just completely added up. I remember I was moving some stuff yet again into a new apartment. When I twisted myself to set the box down my back completely went out on me. Never in my life had I had my back go out so badly. I could barely move. It took me about 30 minutes to get myself off of the floor to get to the bathroom. I was literally at a kind of rock bottom, staring up at the ceiling and wondering what the hell I was doing on this planet. I had no money, no path, I felt useless and was drowning in the deepest grief I had ever known which was subsequently just bringing everything that was wrong up to the surface.

This was before I had even started a real dedicated spiritual practice, but I at that moment decided to reach out to my dad for help. Talking to him gave me comfort, I knew he was around and was desperate to feel and connect with him. I remember sitting on my couch feeling the deepest sorrow. I just sat there in silence, looking out the window asking for help. I asked my dad to help me find my path and purpose, and that I was scared and nervous about the future. Even though I had a master's degree in Sustainable Communities I couldn't bear to bring myself to work in an office. I felt the feeling I had always felt, that I was an outsider and alone in the world unable to relate to the masses. While I was sitting there, staring at the window praying to my dad, my eyes stumbled across a massage table that someone had just placed directly in front of my apartment building on the side of the street.

If that wasn't a sign, I don't know what the hell was. I had gone to massage school back in 2012 but never took the test to get licensed so kind of let it fall to the wayside. I had been doing massage in Alaska because there you didn't actually need a license. While finally exercising my skills in AK I realized the same thing I had realized in school, that I was an incredibly skilled healer. Still, I had dismissed doing massage because I didn't have my national license, but seeing that table, directly in front of my house about 15 minutes after praying to my dad with deep humility, grief, and truth was a freaking sign.

So my sorry ass hobbled out in my robe across the street. I couldn't stand up straight and had a limp but I was determined to get this table. I grabbed it, and it was hella heavy but I dragged it with me across the street, with my back still out, and that was literally the beginning of my healing path. From there one thing led to another, as I began to realize that my dad really was with me guiding me and assisting me, I started to trust the instincts I had about certain things. Because my dad and I are so close in blood, it was like a part of me was almost on the other side as well, a part of me was now non-physical and I was able to identify the signs and signals that he was sending me of where to go and what to do.

One thing led to another until I got to the point of deciding to take the MBLEX test, a national certification for bodyworkers that is accepted across the country. The book to study for this test was about 500 pages long and I forced myself to study as much as I could after getting a full time job as a Wellness

Counselor at a local integrative pharmacy. I made flash cards and did the practice tests. Every time I did them, I was nowhere even near passing. I was and still am an exceptional bodyworker but the rational scientific aspects of the work were never my thing. I'm a feeler and an intuitive. I just know things and where to go and what to do. Having to memorize hundreds of kinesiology questions was starting to wear on me. I was not prepared for a test of this magnitude on top of working my ass of to barely survive.

The day came to take the test. I believe we had 3 hours to complete a 100 question test. When I woke up I consciously chose not to freak out. Instead, I sat at my altar with my dad's chain, a golden amulet of St. Anthony, lit some palo santo and called upon the energies of my dad as well as my beloved massage teacher who had recently died of pancreatic cancer. I said both of their names out loud and asked them to please work through me in this test, help me use my intuition to guide me through the questions with ease. I sat and meditated quietly. Afterwards, I slowly and calmly made my way to the testing facility. Again, when I got there, I lit the palo santo in my car and prayed again to Jim Hackett, my old teacher to guide me as well as my dad, Kenny Buttice. Because I had literally felt my dad around me, I knew that I could begin to access other energies of people I knew and who had touched my life, so I invoked Jim and asked for his assistance and guidance.

The test was very strict and put on by a big testing company. All of us were at our own computers sweating away. Within the first 10 minutes I realized that the entire thing was waaaay over my head. Almost every question that was asked, even though it was a multiple choice, I had absolutely no idea on any one of them. I started to freak out but then just realized that there was no way I was going to pass it with my rational knowledge so I just started going through them as quickly as I could clicking on each answer that felt vaguely familiar. By the time I was done, I was so sure that I had failed that I just got up from my seat and walked out. The woman attendant came to meet me and told me that she could take away my entire test and scores for doing that. I was supposed to call upon her and ask her to come and get me. I was so frustrated and upset I just wanted to get the hell out of there. How was I ever going to pass this test just barely squeaking by, working 40 hours a week and pushing as hard as I can? I was just about to go and ball my eyes out in the car when the woman was able to give me my test results right away. When she handed me the paper I gasped in disbelief. Not only had I passed the test, but I was in the top percentile.

Now this was a bon-a-fide miracle y'all because my ass did *not* consciously know those answers. If I needed yet another sign that I was actually guided, blessed, and protected, here it was. I got into my car and just bawled my eyes out in deep prayer and gratitude to these beings for assisting me on my journey. Getting that license was the major step in becoming the spiritual guide and voice that I am today. Within the year a beautiful office in a brand new building landed in my lap and I started my own practice, *Wild Moon Holistic Bodywork*. This business provided a beautiful platform for me to begin the healing work I was meant to do on this planet. Allowing myself to be open and receptive to the subtle cues of these soul energies that are around me assisting and elevating me has completely shifted my life and helped me tune into my higher purpose.

I tell you this story so that you too can begin to open up to the guidance from your ancestors and those that have passed into the other realm. The truth is that these beings are always with you and if you call on them for assistance in whatever it is that you are having challenges with, if it is in the name of healing and love, they will come to assist you.

Journal Prompts

- What does beginning to cultivate a living, breathing relationship with Spirit world make you feel like?
- Do you think it is possible for you? Or only relegated to the few that have a "gift"?
- Have you had paranormal or mystical experiences in your life? Did they make you conscious of a reality beyond the five senses? Does this scare you? Excite you?
- Do you feel like this is a realm you can exist within, or are you afraid of it?
- Is there anyone close to you that has passed that you feel connected to? How do you feel about calling on them during this time of psychic attunement to help you with your growing sensitivities?

WITCHY BITCH WISDOM

- Intuition can only work through our feelings and through bodily sensations. When you tap into your truth and power, gut and instinct, you'll become more aligned with the truth of who you are.
- The altar is the first step in actually creating a literal and figurative space for yourself in your life that is singularly dedicated to your inner voice, intuition, and connection to a force that is greater than yourself.

- Women and most empaths have been trained since birth to give. Because the masculine/yang energies have been much more valued, women/yin have been trained for millennia to serve that energy. What eventually happened through was that person actually gained their sense of self-worth through the act of giving; this meant that to receive actually made one feel kind of shameful, as if that person wasn't doing her job right.
- This toxic over-giving pattern is one of the biggest challenges in overcoming constantly feeling depleted and exhausted.
- When we pray, we open up our most vulnerable self. Praying is so intimate and liberating. When you start to believe and trust and cultivate this force of love in your life, you'll realize that you can begin to expose yourself to it so it may assist you in true transformation.
- When we start being more truthful with ourselves, we develop a deeper sense of integrity as we allow ourselves to acknowledge the things that are not working for us and maybe never have.

Endnotes

1. Anita Moorjani, *Dying to Be Me* (Carlsbad:: Hay House, 2022)

2

Finding the Flow: Accessing + Opening to your Divine Intuitive Power

> "Intuition is really a sudden immersion of the soul into the universal current of life."
> ~Paulo Coelho, *The Alchemist*

Intuition is the sacred core of our Witch/Queen/Goddess power and the gateway through which all our psychic powers develop. But what the heck is intuition exactly? That's what we'll be exploring this week—tuning into those quiet nudges and whispers that guide us.

Probably the best way to describe intuition is an elusive feeling. Something that you can't quite put your finger on. It is of the feminine realm, deep inside, mysterious, and internal. It can be as subtle as the bare inkling of a feeling that something doesn't feel quite right. Or an alarm inside your body that says, "Get the hell out of here now." Essentially, intuition is how the force of love and beauty and goodness that animates this universe works through us to guide us. **Because most of us are accustomed to living in a world guided by control and rationality instead of what we "feel" to be right, we have been led down a long, dark path of "shoulds."** As we explored in Week 1, the shoulds defy our feelings (our truth) and get us nowhere. They only perpetuate the darkness inside us, making us more and more blind to ourselves.

I have seen so many people come through my office that feel lost. They feel exhausted and depleted, anxious and depressed and they can't see a way out. They are tired but the deepest most profound loss they communicate to me is an inability to access their truth. When we are in tune with our truth, essentially our deep gut feeling about something, we are in tune with which direction to go in life. It's those deep guttural feelings of the "uh-huh" or "nuh-uh" that guide us in the right direction. Because almost none of us have been taught to open to the spirit realm (which is where this feeling lives) or been given permission to outside of religion, many of us who aren't religious are lost, unable to tune into which way is the right way. This results in a crippling kind of anxiety that has no bare end or a kind of depression that no kind of pure joy can heal. On the flip-side, it can result in a kind of emptiness that can lead one down a path of the insatiable need for more, more money, drugs, plastic surgery, etc. There is a palpable emptiness that one is unable to feel, or does feel and it shows itself as anxiety, depression, greed, or the constant need to be "doing."

What I find over and over and over is that the women who come to see me are incredibly intuitive, meaning they can sense what is going on with others and in turn feel obligated to help them, because they can feel their pain. Yet, the intuitive voice works both ways, it can give us a feeling about someone but it also gives us direct guidance in our own lives. **What I have found is that these women will use their intuition and empathy to assist and enhance the lives of others but when that same voice guides them on their own truth and path, they dismiss it. What ends up happening is that these women become door-mats, they give and give and give to a point of feeling utterly exhausted and depleted and then because of this end up carrying within them a deep well of resentment because they are so empty from over-giving.** I know these women well because I was this woman. What I am actively healing in myself, I help others heal in themselves, we are all on this journey together.

Women + empaths have been the caretakers, mothers, servants, and maids for millennia. But there is a deeper energetic patterning here, and that is the feminine energy of the world, serving masculine energy. This is part of our collective consciousness that we are all a part of. It is the imbalance of feminine energy that has led to our power and beauty getting relegated to the role of "caretaker." This isn't, of course, ALL women everywhere. I am speaking of collective energy that we have internalized for eons. This is beyond real. It is so real it lives in the bones of our mother's mothers. We are finally at a point in time, here in our herstory where feminine *power*, the intuitive and feeling energy that we carry inside of us can be seen and venerated for what it is. It is this power, in fact, that is going to change the energy of the planet. But as I have said many times, it literally starts with us, and what does that mean? It means that when we get intuitive information regarding our own lives and our own path that we choose to *follow* it.

We have been using our power, insight, feeling, and empathy to serve everyone else but ourselves. We give and give. We serve and serve. We do much of the emotional labor for our partners, family, and friends and take on their pain. Yet when it comes to our own pain, our own process, our own truth, we deny it. Why? Because that is what we were taught. For eons, women have gathered their sense of self-worth from serving. A woman's place was in the home, and this meant that in order for her as her own being on this planet to feel power, serving her family well brought her the greatest satisfaction. Because a woman's work has been based in service, giving is what brought her worth. This made it incredibly uncomfortable for her to receive because traditionally if she was receiving she wasn't doing her job well.

What I am doing here is talking about the archetype, (a collective subconscious energy that runs throughout all of humanity and all of its cultures) that is psychically embedded in the consciousness of women and anyone that is overly empathic. I have seen this over and over, and in order for us to fully begin to viscerally feel and begin to exercise our sacred power, it's imperative we understand what has kept us back.

I have felt this collective subconscious energy deep in my bones for years. As a half-Italian, curvaceous woman, I definitely have the Mama Mia archetype. I have come to realize that in a world that doesn't value the subtle energetic + intuitive realm of the feminine, the thing that made me feel most powerful with gifts unseen was to give.

I have come to realize that in a world that doesn't value the subtle energetic + intuitive realm of the feminine, the thing that made me feel most powerful with gifts unseen was to give.

These gifts of sensitivity and deep knowing exist, which means that I am able to sense the shadow of others, what they themselves need, even if they are not admitting it to themselves outright. I would listen to those close to me and do everything I could to fix their problems because feeling useful was how I gathered my sense of self-worth. I felt that at least in some way, I was using my natural born gifts. Yet, I began to notice as I got older and became more self-aware that I was meddling in places I wasn't invited. I would almost seek out what was happening with people deep down when they weren't ready or willing to talk about it. When those people wouldn't open up to me, I felt like I hadn't done my job and felt worthless. It would bring me back to having to face my own sense of self and lack of self-worth which was very low. This pattern continued for many years. This resulted in a constant state of over-giving and resentment from those who didn't want me involved or taking the energy I was giving and getting nothing in return. This perpetuated my deep well of anger and resentment and fueled my unworthiness even more. This was exactly like your typical overbearing Italian mother archetype. Ugh. This is also where the Witches of the world go when they have no outlet to express themselves or their healing gifts of intuitive sight, magic, and healing.

Journal Prompts

- Do you have patterns of over-giving in your own life? Does your mother?
- Do you feel there are times when you are not authentically giving? Or when you give out of duty versus true desire? Can you distinguish between the two?

- Do you hold onto resentment for having to give so much to those around you? How can you begin to balance this with receiving?
- Do you trust the intuitive wisdom you receive about your own life?

The Sacred Sense

If you are reading this, I am guessing that you are highly empathic and intuitive. These two powers go together as what they really are is a heightened sense of sensitivity. And usually, it comes down to just *knowing* something without having any idea how the hell you know it. Where does this *knowing* come from and what the hell is it? It's our sacred power y'all, it's our Witch power and the more we focus on it, empower it, and trust it, the stronger it becomes.

Our intuition is the entryway into all other psychic powers and at its most basic it is a feeling that we receive about something. The feeling resides in our bodies, it doesn't reside in our heads. The feeling is a hunch, an inkling, a sense. That is precisely what it is, another sense. It is not something that can be measured or seen, so when trying to defend it against rationality, it will always lose.

This sense is based on our sensitivity. This is where, for the first time in our lives, within a culture that banks on stuffing our truth and power aside to fit into what is rational and productive, we don't. More sensitivity is exactly what this world needs and we empaths are the ones to usher in this new era.

Being sensitive means that you are highly conscious, it means that you have a higher level of awareness of what is happening around you and that you take in that energy

completely—that you are receptive. You are not simply operating from your rational mind, you are operating from your entire being, meaning that you are able to sense and feel what is happening within the environment and people around you. This can be incredibly intense within a world that is cruel in so many ways. But it's incredibly rewarding as well as you are so much more connected with all of life. Because the paradigm at large has seen this deep connection with all of life as a weakness or simply not seen it at all, we Witches have felt weak, inundated with grief, and unable to see ourselves as the powerful beings that we truly are.

Every human is born sensitive and whole, using our intuition and our brains in equal measure, but little by little we are trained out of it. Carl Jung said it well when he said that "Modern [wo]man suffered from an atrophy of instinct[1]."Our instincts are the most basic of our intuition. It's what animals use to navigate their way to a hunt, and it's something that we still carry within us on a deep primordial level. It's our raw wild nature. Ever have an experience where you are in a crowded place and you just unconsciously turn your head directly to see someone staring at you? That is an instinct, where the body takes over and we aren't even fully aware of what we are doing. **Intuition is just heightened instinct. Yet because of the imbalance of rational vs. intuitive energy on this planet, we have all but lost this natural drive that we carry that is ultimately the deeper universal psychic Spirit working through us. We have become so inundated with rationality, we have forgotten the powerful and lost art of *feeling* if something is right or not.**

Intuition is just heightened instinct

Intuition begins with a feeling and it can only increase when we begin to trust the feeling. If we do not trust the feeling than that means we ignore our inner voice and we dismiss our own wild nature. Intuition is the wild rhythm of the divine working itself through us. As we are trained out of trusting it, we are trained out of our own true nature. Despite what we have been taught and conditioned into, we are not apart from the wild, we are a part of it. Our human *nature* when allowed to express itself fully is in tune with a deeper, natural rhythm that is naturally guided. Because we have been trained out of honoring our own nature, we have lost this connection. This is when the rational "mind" that is connected to the mass consciousness of "should" takes over and we depart from our natural truth. So many of us are getting guided everyday but because this guidance makes no *sense* we ignore it, only to be thrown directly back into the machine of doing, doing, doing and feeling exhausted, depleted, and lost.

When we begin to use our intuition as our main guidance system in life, we in turn become our own source. We allow ourselves and our consciousness to merge with universal life force energy. We no longer are a slave to the system at large, hoping to keep up and doing everything we can to maintain our power. Instead, we become so much more. When we begin to use our intuition, the sacred space within us that is connected to universal life force energy, that feels the wild pulse of life on this planet and allows this cosmic energy to flow through us, we, in turn, become our own source. When we see this as a power instead of a weakness we are actively reshaping the energy of this planet.

Journal Prompts

- Have you been made to feel ashamed of your sensitivity?
- Has your sensitivity been something you have hidden from others in your life?
- Have you ever seen your sensitivity as a power? Have you ever linked it to your intuition?

Becoming Your Own Source

What do I mean when I say "becoming one's own source"? As I said earlier, the feminine energy of this planet has been serving the masculine for eons, and what that has created is generally women looking to men as their *source*, meaning their source of money, validation, safety, etc. And rightfully so, it has been a very masculinized world where those powers were solely offered to men and men only. It's not just men, but the masculine structures that have built this world. It's the hierarchical institutions and the bureaucratic coldness that this *structure* has offered us all something to lean on. For women and for the feminine energy of this planet, there has been little to believe in to keep one safe that is outside of this system. Until now. The times they are a changin y'all and the feminine is breaking through. This is visible to us in the world as we see women of all colors paving a new path in politics, music, movies, literature, science, etc. **But what I am really talking about here is the energy of the Divine, the etheric, the Spiritual realm, which is the realm of the feminine. As we begin to open up to this energy which means engaging with it on the daily, believing in it, holding it, and seeing it show up for us again and again we are making this energy our *source* instead of any human or any structure that we may believe will keep us safe.**

When we know that we are taken care of, held, and protected

by a deeper guiding force in this world, we begin to know deep in our bones that this is the source of everything, and we no longer need to seek anything from anyone outside.

This is the moment that I believe a woman becomes a true woman, as she is not needing anything other than the Divine to guide her and so she reclaims her sovereignty and also her fear, choosing faith, courage, and deep internal connection over all else.

Intuition can guide us very subtly or very intensely. I have found that the more awake I become, if I am able to identify my intuition and I, in turn, do not follow it, the louder the messages will become. I cannot tell you the number of times I have been in a situation that I knew I shouldn't be in. Yet, instead of using my voice to express this and get myself out of it, I went against my *OWN INNER AUTHORITY*, my intuition. The stronger the feeling became that I shouldn't be in that situation and the more I did not honor that feeling, the stronger the signs got.

Spirit really comes to knock me down and show me the way especially when I'm in relationships I shouldn't be in. I remember getting back together with an ex-boyfriend that I had been on and off with for years. You already know where this is heading, getting back together with ex's almost never works out but how many of us have done it because we fear being alone, amidst many other reasons. This was why I chose to get back together with my ex-boyfriend named Luke. We had broken up and gotten back together so many times it was becoming kind of a joke. The only person the joke was being played on was me though. I *knew* we weren't right for each other but he had so many qualities that I wanted. He was funny, fun, adventurous, he cared, he saw my power, and on top of it we had incredible sex. I was *always* able to rationalize myself into getting back together with him by saying something like, "No one knows me like him" or "He has been doing a lot of work on himself to change" or "I've done a lot of work on myself to change, it's a two-way street." And yes, these were some rational truths that could be argued but the deeper feeling I had within myself was that he wasn't the right match. I had yet to truly enter my true Witch power though and was still operating from so many wounds in myself, I was not able to trust myself. I dare not access this truth though, because that would mean I would have to face myself on a deeper level and face the fact that I was completely alone. That meant I would have to confront the deep pain and fear that being alone brought up in me, and I wasn't ready to do that, at least not yet. I still wanted what I wanted and I was pushing through, pushing for some "American Ideal" that was never my path. There were so many truths I wasn't ready to own up to yet, so much darkness I was afraid of in myself.

I remember deciding to get back together with Luke back in the fall of 2014. I drove all the way from Flagstaff, Arizona to Anchorage, Alaska in my 1995 Nissan Pathfinder. That truck was awesome. I had just finished two years of graduate school; I had completed a master's degree in Sustainable Communities and it had been one of the roughest periods of my life. Talk about patriarchal structures that numb out all intuitive knowing and feeling, Jesus. Even though this program was very alternative and studied all the collective reasons for why our world is the way it is and how we can change it, it still operated within a hierarchical, patriarchal institution which bred a kind of catty competitive environment that was soul-sucking to me.

After graduate school, the time had come that I was going to be moving on from Flagstaff. I needed an adventure after my soul had been tied up in a pit of loneliness, depression, and insanity for the past 2 years and Luke, the wild man that he was, offering me an out. So I took it. He came and met me in San Francisco and drove the rest of the way with me up to Anchorage. I remember seeing him for the first time and just laughing and laughing. He was an old friend so it was always great to revisit with him. Well, that fun lasted about a week because by the time we had gotten into Canada and were on our 4th-day driving, some signs were emerging that I hadn't wanted to face.

At this point on our 4th day, we were at the very top of the northern territory of British Columbia, where no one lives, and I mean NO ONE. It had started snowing and we were driving a truck that was 19 years old with about 175,000 miles on it. It was dark outside and there were no lights...anywhere. There was no one for miles upon miles, it was the kind of place where if you got stranded, you would die. I was craving wildness, and here it was, smack dab in front of my face. It was in that dark evening drive where the snow was coming down and I could barely see 5 feet in front of me that Luke and I began arguing. I'm not even sure about what, it was a replay of the same argument we had a thousand times before. I remember the singular instance where my stomach dropped and I thought, "I'm making the wrong decision." But there was no turning back. I had gone against my intuition and now with no money, no family, and no job, I had no way of turning back. There I was going farther and farther into a dark abyss with him.

What ensued was to be one of the darkest years of my life. I had gotten back together with Luke out of fear and because of that, I was met with my own darkness, literally. Obviously, I like to put myself through extreme situations in order to learn my freaking lesson, but my god, this one was really intense. By the time February came rolling around I was going insane. Luke would do everything he could to make me happy, buy me whatever I wanted, take me on trips, but the darkness was so palpable inside of me and unnameable that I couldn't even put words to it. I just remember him taking me out to the fanciest restaurant in Anchorage on the top floor of the fanciest hotel in the middle of the Alaskan winter. We had this window seat and I remember looking out the window at the full moon shining above us. We had everything one could want- food, sex, and money, but I was so empty. I was trying to describe to him the darkness inside of me at that dinner and could barely get the words out. All I could do was stare at the moon, the symbol of the deep feminine itself and its giant beautiful face lighting the tears streaming down my face. I remember the maître-d coming over to assist us in whatever we needed and tears were running down my cheeks, he looked at me like "Get your shit together lady." That wasn't the place to lose your shit, but I was losing my shit all over town. I was losing my shit because I was betraying the truth of myself. I was betraying my soul. I was so lost. Because of the denial of the truth, I had no faith, no trust, and no connection. I literally wanted to die.

Around this time, I remember sitting at my altar and praying on my hands and knees, asking God to help me. I had the instinct to pick up one of my favorite books, *Women Who Run with Wolves*[2] and use it as an oracle, as almost every word of that book could be seen as a sacred kind of guidance in that magical piece of literature. I remember opening it up to a passage about how women will wither away when kept in any kind of cage or relationship that holds her natural power back. The message was clear as day, "get the hell out of here" it said. It was at that moment I realized I needed to leave Luke, somehow. I finally took the wool from over my eyes and decided to look at the facts of my life with deep truth. I hadn't up until this point believed I could make it on my own and in many ways, I simply didn't want to make it on my own. But my soul was telling me I must listen to my intuition, my gut, and my higher self, and finally I did. From that point on, I started looking for work, any work. Eventually, I got a job at a reputable chiropractor's office making the most money I had ever made in my life. I moved out of the shared house with Luke I had in Anchorage and into my own cabin in the woods that I had wanted since I moved to Alaska. This crisis point and the direct communication and intention for help from Spirit put me on the healing path I am on today.

Journal Prompts

- Having grown up in a culture where the source of God was always outside of you, what does it feel like to believe that source is actually you?
- Does it frighten you? Does it empower you? Is it awkward?
- Reflect on your answers deeply and begin reconciling with the realization that there is NO-THING outside of yourself. It all resides within you!

Making Space for Yourself

Because we women and men have all been part of this incredible imbalance of masculine and feminine energy for so many years, it has led us to all of us, especially women to ignore our inner voice and intuition. Nothing and no one has ever taught us to value it. In school, we are taught to read, write, do math, exercise, but are we taught to listen to our inner voice and guidance? No. We are directed towards all of the external material creations, the masculine energies of externalization, materialism, control, and rationality. Yet those more subtle internal voices and feelings, that energy that is of the Spirit realm has never been seen as being "worth" anything. In fact, it's actually been seen as being silly, irrelevant, irrational, weak, make-believe, impossible, and dangerous. The list goes on and on and on. No wonder why us sensitives and empaths have had such a hard time discovering our true power and worth. It's something that has never been part of the equation. Until now.

I will repeat this over and over in this book, as it is the crux of recognizing, building, and sitting inside of our true self-worth. **In order for our Everyday Witch power to come out of the closet, we must begin to *trust* the inner wisdom Spirit is giving us. This is our own true nature begging to be witnessed. Yet because so many of us have been trained out of recognizing this guidance, which is our birthright and a natural part of being human, we feel lost and alone. The thing is, learning to trust these feelings we get from the world around us and within us actually means that we begin to trust ourselves.** *This is huge.* In this world, we have been trained not to trust ourselves. It makes sense within a patriarchy that women shouldn't trust their inner voice, and that they need men in order to be able to function properly. A patriarchal system couldn't maintain its balance of power without that energy. Because feminine wisdom hasn't been validated or seen as real, men have had the upper hand on the "rational" realm. This may not even be what those men themselves wanted, they could have been born incredibly intuitive and sensitive yet because the culture at large demands their strength and numbness, they had to remove that part of themselves in order to fit in, just as women that contain dominant masculine energies have had to downplay that part of themselves. No one wins in this system.

This is what has perpetuated the infantilization of women. Women have come so far on this planet but because of the years upon years of needing to get male approval, it has led to an energetic weakness in us trusting in the Spirit realm, in our own power, and the feelings within. This has kept us small, very small, to the point that we feel bad taking up any space at all. **In order to get into the rink and compete, we have to "perform" within this circus, either adopting one or the other heteronormative role of a desirable female or tough female. Nowhere in this equation, are we able to be ourselves.**

When we start to open up to the truth of ourselves, meaning beginning to excavate, honor, and bow to what we are genuinely feeling in any given moment, we become real women. We rise into the High Priestesses that we are. Simply put, we begin to mature. So many of us have been lost for years and years, I know I was. There was always this deep wound inside of me that felt that I needed the love of a man in order to feel complete. Having a father that wasn't ever really present with me left a big vacant hole in my life, always vying for the attention of males yet never hitting the mark. Because of the PWC in which men carry the power and the influence, to not have that attention from my father just accelerated the worthlessness inside of me. Even though I presented everywhere in my life as a very confident and strong Italian woman, inside I still felt like a little girl reacting endlessly from the deep wounds within.

When we excavate, honor, and bow to what we genuinely feel

at any given moment, we become real women. We rise into the High Priestesses that we are. Simply put, we mature.

I never fully woke up to this truth until one day when I was well into my 30's, at my altar once again praying and processing over a man that I had lost from my life. I was praying and crying, and at one point I just stopped and said out loud, "This doesn't feel right anymore." It's like the part of me that was crying was still that little girl, wounded and alone, desperately needing her daddy to come and give her attention. And this is what we don't fully address within the PWC; if we have not fully matured into women the men in our lives are in some way a kind of father/paternal figure to us. This is what this imbalanced energy has placed onto these men, so much responsibility towards the woman. Patriarchy has led to men being the voice of reason against our irrational and uncertain inner world, a world we ourselves have been taught to fear, a world too powerful for us to be able to handle. Until now.

That day, I literally stopped crying in my tracks and I realized something. I had come too far in my development of myself to cry like that any longer. Crying like that felt like I was still a little girl, and I was no longer that little girl anymore. The reason I wasn't, was because I began to honor and trust myself as the High Priestess that I truly am. What this meant, was that I had done enough work excavating my inner truth to begin to surrender my fears and beliefs about whatever the hell it was in my life that I believed I wanted in order for me to be "happy" which generally meant "safe." Instead I began to trust my intuition more than my own mind.

This one event changed me. I began to sit up straighter and to hold myself differently. Instead of concave chest and shoulders, my heart was out, my shoulders held back. I began to hold my head a little higher, and feel a little more powerful. **I had transformed into a woman, a high priestess who was so in tune with the rhythms of nature and trusting in this power, no longer needed approval from the outside world to understand where to go in life. I didn't need to look to the men in my life or the hierarchical structures to engage in the truth of who I was. I was a goddamn Queen, a High Priestess in her own right and as I began to truly honor and bow to that energy within me, I began to see myself and body as the sacred and incredible vessel that it is.** I am the Divine Feminine incarnate, I am holy, I am the Earth, I am Spirit. I am literally a channel for this force of love to work through so that this earth can begin to heal, rebalance, and re-own feminine energy as it once was— and so are you.

I am the Divine Feminine Incarnate, I am holy, I am Earth, I am Spirit.

This was quite the difference from the little girl consciousness I had been operating from my entire life. The little girl that was afraid never felt good enough, felt worthless and unlovable. The little girl that was constantly needing other people's approval in order to feel worthy and safe. The little girl that was constantly looking outside of herself in order to be directed. Beginning to own your true Everyday Witch power is beginning to disengage with the culture at large that breeds fear and scarcity and begin to tap the well of beauty that comes from within. We have the raging river of the divine feminine running through every one of our veins and it is this force that when tapped, engaged, and honored that will begin to guide, empower, and make us into the *true women* that we are, with our heads held high. **It is our time to rise, just as it is our time to begin to lead and shift the energies of this planet, and it begins with us recognizing the divinity that courses through our own veins and the dark well of mystery that guides our every move. It's time magic begins to return to this earth, the miraculous, and the things that are explainable. Only when you begin to trust in this force will the magic and power begin to appear in your life.**

Transforming into the High Priestess that I am was not a transformation that happened overnight, but ever so slowly. As I began to cultivate a living and breathing relationship with Spirit, I simultaneously became incredibly open to its signs and signals. I felt the natural world speaking through me and to me every day. It came in all kinds of ways, a sign on the side of a truck, a song that came on the radio, a random idea that popped into my head out of nowhere, feeling led to take a different route home, saying no to clients I had no desire to work with any longer— the list goes on and on. Little by little, as I began to trust the subtle cues I was getting from Spirit, over and over— the strength, connection, and power within me grew. I began to understand that the synchronicities I was experiencing weren't some random coincidence but pure guidance and illumination. When I started to open myself to paying more attention to how I felt at any certain moment and allowed myself to fully surrender to that moment through my attention, I would automatically become more present.

This means that I had developed a relationship with Universal life force energy, focused, and cultivated my connection to this force so intensely that I began to be led by a subtle, quiet, yet incredibly potent force. This happened because I chose to become more conscious and aware of this force by believing

in it and then allowing it to guide me. This guidance cannot in any way happen without TRUSTING the information you are getting from Spirit. There is no power without the trust y'all.

Journal Prompts

- Using the definition I have just outlined, do you feel like you have matured into a "woman" (age has nothing to do with this)?
- Is there any kind of "little girl" consciousness you still carry within yourself?
- Are there any parts that feel you need approval or validation to feel okay?

Letting Go: Relinquishing Fear

Let's get into this. This shit ain't easy, especially for us women. We have been deeply enculturated to be in a constant state of fear; our bodies carry a deep collective pain that is tense and on high alert at all times. I cannot tell you how deeply I feel the truth of this. As a High Priestess myself, I believe it is this sacred power that we carry that actually processes the energies of the planet. And I will tell you, as I began to open to Spirit and begin to LET GO of all that fear holding me together, whoooooeeeeeeeeee did I have a nervous breakdown.

I have always lived incredibly free and rebellious, probably to a fault. That whole rock-n-roll lifestyle really did apply to my family and I was a child with, let's just say, very limited supervision. My mom is an Aquarius and had very little interest in disciplining or telling me what to do. By the time I was 13 years old, I was feisty. I *really* didn't like anyone telling me what to do, in fact, I had a visceral reaction to it. I had no problem telling my friends' parents off if they were overstepping their bounds on my freedom. I was wild, and stayed wild for years. I was never fully domesticated.

Still, as free and alive and rebellious as I remember myself being, getting older and facing myself, truly facing myself with the assistance of Spirit felt like I was going insane. What I came up against was facing the extent to which I was trying to control my external reality in order to feel safe. Because let's face it, that is why we control anything. We "control" as much as we can in order to not be met with any surprises, but really, for us sensitives, I believe control comes down to us doing everything we can to feel safe.

For literally thousands of years women have been afraid of being attacked, beaten, accused, raped, assaulted—the list goes on and on and on. As I started doing this work, sitting with the deepest humility, grief, and truth at my altar to face the Divine completely naked– man was I met with my deepest fears. As the moment came for me to surrender, which meant letting go of whatever it was that I thought I was doing to maintain my reality, man oh man was I met face to face with this cellular encased tension that felt like an ice block. As I would sit there and meditate, I felt the tension moving all throughout my body, letting go was physically painful. **Letting go meant that I had to trust in a world that has *never* had my back. We women hold ourselves tightly because we have *had to*. We have had to be on guard, watching, always watching. This tightness and tension, this fear of releasing this grip that we have held so tightly in order to be kept safe is no longer what is keeping us safe any more, it is actually making us sick.**

I have seen this so many times in so many of my clients. It

seems like the more "successful" in this mad world they are, the more they seem to have things "under control." It is these women especially that would come to me for massages and to talk out their feelings—but try and approach them about learning to surrender their ironclad grip on whatever it was they were doing, I would risk getting my head chopped off. There was always a fine line that I could not cross with these women where the second I would approach the topic of offering and begin to loosen their grip so Spirit could do its thing they would turn on me, hiss at me, and show their fangs. "NO WAY IN HELL BITCH" is what they were essentially saying.

One of my clients in particular, Lila, whom I had worked with for years, would go through this same cycle over and over again. She had had an incredibly traumatic childhood, watching her mom get beaten over and over and with her step dad telling her daily that she was an ugly piece of shit. She grew up in a trailer and was now having to take care of her mostly absent father who was dying of dementia and constantly verbally abusing her. This woman was incredible, she did not let any of this keep her from creating the life she wanted. She had a thriving business with her husband, who was a beautiful man, and a beautiful daughter who was very awake. The thing about Lila was that every week she would come in with the same issues— insomnia, a kind of perpetual state of tension that most people would collapse from, migraines, exhaustion, the list goes on and on. Lila could not delegate any responsibility to anyone because she didn't trust anyone. She carried all of the weight and all of the burden herself so that she knew she was safe, keeping it all under control. Every week Lila would come in, some weeks she was great, others she was having a breakdown but it was always the same persistent idea of letting go, that if

I even broached it, the fangs would come out silently saying, "STEP OFF BITCH, I'M IN CONTROL."

Lila would tell me over and over how much I had changed her life and how she had never met anyone like me before who was able to help her in the way that I have; yet the second I would talk about releasing control, she would completely shut down. To her, the control was what kept her safe— it kept her in power, in command. Yet it wore on her day in and day out, so much so that at 35 her hair was nearly all grey. No one dared know that though, she had that shit on lock and UNDER CONTROL. It was a dark pitch black to the naked eye.

This kind of control, which is essentially fear, is why we get sick. Stress wears on us sensitives, and it's no wonder why the most empathic ones seem to get sick so easily. We are incredibly sensitive, no matter how thick an armor we carry. And to be holding our bodies as tightly as we do day in and day out, keeping our minds and spirits in a state of perpetual fear, it wears on our immune system, our body, and literally our spirit. Absorbing this fear after years and years begins to wear on you. And the more sensitive you are, the more exhausted, depleted, and tired you will feel.

I want to make sure you understand that this is NOT our fault. We are living in a world that perpetuates fear in order to maintain control. But that is the thing, if we can begin to learn to trust instead of fear, we begin to flip this entire system on its head. We create a revolution from deep within and return as the sacred channels of Spirit that we have always been. The Divine Feminine incarnate, the Witches of the world, the High Priestesses uniting in order to reclaim our true power.

Releasing control and beginning a practice of sacred trust is the antidote to the ills of our world. It calms the immune system and let's go of the burden of having to handle it all on our own. This is where the true source of power lies, and from where the core of intuition is born.

Journal Prompts

- What is your relationship with control?
- How does it make you feel to think about letting go of control? Does it give you relief or stress you out?
- How has the process of praying and offering been going for you? Do you feel yourself loosening? What is the most challenging? What comes easiest?

Paradox

It's normal to believe that we are keeping ourselves safe by holding on tight to what we believe is safety, i.e., keeping things under control. But this is based on the belief that our human selves are running this show; the old triangular paradigm within a hierarchy and patriarchy— with one person at the top, one winner, and one thing as superior. However, the emerging paradigm of the Divine Feminine is led by paradox, with two seeming opposites simultaneously being true. With paradox, there is no right or wrong. There is no black or white. It's not one or the other; it's both, honey. One or the other is linear, as is a hierarchy. But the truth is that reality is everything, everywhere at once. It is, in fact, NOT linear; it's quantum. Within the realm of the Divine Fem, it's both baby. When we embrace paradox as the truth of our reality, we actually begin to let go of what is right and wrong—the exact thinking that perpetuates our fear. **The PWC, with its male god at the top,** has convinced us there is one good energy and one bad energy. And this linear and dualistic thinking has had an energetic influence over every system, science, and thinking that has preceded it. It has led to us spending our entire lives trying not to be bad.

So what the hell does beginning to embrace paradox look like in our lives? Your journey will be unique to you, but for me, this concept was incredibly liberating because I'm a Virgo—a sign known for perfectionism or wanting to be "good" all the time. When I embraced the paradox, I began to embrace those aspects of me that were imperfect and didn't completely fit into any box. I gave myself space to be more than one thing. Embracing paradox meant eliminating that flawless, shiny exterior and accepting my own darkness, my own imperfections. It gave me permission to be it all.

To embrace our darkness is to allow ourselves to be whole. We have become splintered in this modern era, putting ap-pearances above authenticity. Much of the time, our authen-tic truth is dark, i.e difficult or unappealing to others and ourselves. So we avoid it, we sweep it under the rug, we do everything we can to pretend it doesn't exist, but the funny thing is that our darkness is the yin part of ourselves, it's where the truth lives. And the truth is also aligned with our intuition, deep inside of the belly. This is part of the great mystery of life. Because so many of us have denied our own darkness, we have in turn denied our authentic selves and sent ourselves the message that our truth is not worthy or "good."

Paradox: the ability to hold two contradictory forces as being of equal value and worth. The world we live in today is breaking because of the collective inability to hold paradox; that more than one thing can simultaneously be true. We create wars of right and wrong. And all of this external war is what happens inside of the self as well. We sanitize and hide the parts of ourselves we don't feel are palatable, and through that we ever so slowly lose touch with what our truth is. Remember that intuition + truth reside in the darkness, and without the acknowledgment and honoring of this energy that resides inside and outside of ourselves, we become lost.

Journaling Prompts

- How does it feel to begin to view your world in terms of paradox? Is it difficult?
- How does it feel to begin reconciling that there is no "bad?" Can you get down with that? Does it fry your circuit board? Does it free you?

Embodiment

Everything about beginning to live from your own intuitive center instead of from your mind points to us beginning to live our lives from the body instead of head. This seems easy enough to grasp, but let me explain why it's revolutionary.

The entire culture of the PWC has literally made us disembodied, meaning that we have not been integrating our body in our daily living experience. Disembodiment has made us direct and guide our lives from a rational standpoint, our head. We use our minds to decide *if* something should be done, *how* it should be done, *when* it should be done etc. When we use our mind to make decisions from this place, we are reacting to the culture at large. We are essentially making choices from the consciousness of a system that is innately

sick and off balanced. We are not integrating our other senses or other ways of knowing. As Carl Jung pointed out, we have many different ways of knowing things, thinking only being *one* of those ways. Because we discount other ways of knowing, we have cut ourselves off from a deeper, more nuanced, and textured life. It's as if we cut ourselves off from other parts of our innate intelligence that our ancestors had access to. We are living dis-integrated from our senses, and because of that what our body senses as real, valued, and worthy has been unable to be acknowledged because it is irrational. This has neutered our identities.

What ends up happening through this process is that we disregard any information that we are getting from our body, from our heart and our gut, from our pelvis– all living breathing parts of our entire being. We have been trained that the brain is separate from our bodies; again embracing that dualistic way of being. If we want to truly tap into our power and find our authentic truth, purpose, and power, we must begin to integrate the wisdom that is of another paradigm, thus the wisdom of the body and of the spirit.

The paradigm of the feminine is an embodied knowledge, meaning that we integrate our minds and bodies in the move-ment of our lives. When we are operating from our mind only as we have been taught to do in this culture, we disregard the wisdom of the heart and gut which is where our feeling self is centered. This is where our intuition lives. This is how we have gotten to where we are today on planet earth with so much numbness and desensitization. Most humans have learned to disengage from that part of themselves which has diverted from their inner knowing. One can only perpetuate this state if one IS in fact disembodied, to be fully embodied and remain completely numb isn't fully possible. Our feeling realm is the realm of the body, and as we begin to open up to it, we realign with the truth of ourselves. The withdrawal of feminine power and wisdom has led to a deficiency of intuition in our mainstream culture. This is where the heart of creativity and authenticity live.

Imagine for a moment that living from our heads only is akin to living a life that is in black and white. The black and the white is the dualistic paradigm of the PWC, and has a clearly placed definition and place for things— it being one or the other. When operating from this space, we are only able to engage so much of our consciousness. We are limited to what we are able to conceive of because we are not integrating the opposing energy. It keeps us in our own box. This box is what has been presented to us as "normal" and, if we decide to venture out of this box we are going to be incredibly different; we run the risk of not belonging. Yet still, we feel unsatisfied with the confines within which we have been given to operate. We feel stifled, bored, and honestly lost, unable to access what is true for us. This is what living from only our mind is like. We have a scope of what is accepted and possible for us and we live our lives defined and controlled by that "status quo" without ever fully waking up to the fact that this status quo is perpetuating a kind of psychic death. Consciousness never stops expanding no matter how controlled we try and keep our lives. Staying inside of our black and white world of the mind for someone constantly evolving is like living in a kind of prison with no bars.

Now imagine this world was imbued with every color of the rainbow. And all of a sudden, our consciousness was able to pick up on minute subtleties of things that we had never noticed before; nuance. This in turn affects us, it affects our consciousness and moves our being. It inspires us and provokes us to express, feel, and tune into our environment even more. It opens us up to see the other side of things and to embrace opposites. Because the color is so incredible and multi-dimensional, we reflect this. We begin to feel more, are moved by beauty and realize that we are feeling everything a little bit deeper. We sense the interconnection between everything and can viscerally feel the energy of things. We innately became more present because of how engaging our environment is. This is what beginning to integrate your intuition and the wisdom of the body does for our consciousness, it opens it up to the subtle multi-dimensionality of our entire existence and takes us out of *reacting* and instead opens us up to *allowing*.

Operating from our intuitive core is what makes us more embodied, which allows us to access a much bigger and broader kind of consciousness. It literally takes us out of the prison of black and white duality and brings us into a world of color where we begin to engage with life on a completely new and powerful level.

Instead of things being "right and wrong" they become a spectrum of possibility all happening at once, a rainbow. Opening ourselves to the truth of our intuition is what brings the color to us, it's where the rainbow operates from. **We no longer have to only operate from the head or the heart, but instead can integrate them both. Two different kinds of consciousness simultaneously working together, paradox. This is the feminine coming out of the closet, becoming seen after being eclipsed for thousands of years.**

Journaling Prompts

- Have you felt disconnected from your heart and gut in your life? Have you used it to guide you, or have you made your decisions more rationally?
- How does this way of living make you feel? Do you feel free and more integrated or awkward and out of control? Are you able to befriend this part of you? Or is it still something on a deep level you are afraid of?
- What draws you to this work? What are you really seeking?

WITCHY BITCH WISDOM

- Women have been the caretakers, mothers, servants, and maids for millennia. There is a deeper energetic patterning here, and that is the feminine energy of the world, serving masculine energy.
- We have been using our power, insight, feeling, and empathy to serve everyone else but ourselves. We give and give. Yet when it comes to our own pain, our own process, our own truth, we deny it. Why? Because that is what we were taught. For eons, women have gathered their sense of self-worth from serving.
- Our intuition is the entryway into all other psychic powers and, at its most basic, it is a feeling that we get. The feeling resides in our bodies, it doesn't reside in our heads. The feeling is a hunch, an inkling, a sense. It is not something that can be measured or seen, so trying to defend it against rationality, it will always lose.
- So many of us are getting guided everyday but because this guidance makes no "sense" we ignore it, only to be thrown directly back into the machine of doing, doing, doing and

64

feeling exhausted, depleted, and lost.

- Because women and men have all been part of this incredible imbalance of masculine and feminine energy for so many years, it has led us to all of us, especially women to ignore our inner voice and intuition.
- It makes sense within a patriarchy that women shouldn't trust their inner voice, and that they need men in order to be able to function properly. A patriarchal system couldn't maintain its balance of power without that energy.
- Beginning to own your true Everyday Witch power is beginning to disengage with the culture at large, which breeds fear and scarcity, and begin to tap the well of beauty that comes from within.
- Releasing control and beginning a practice of sacred trust is the antidote to the ills of our world. It calms the immune system and let's go of the burden of having to handle it all on our own. This is where the true source of power lies, and from where the core of intuition is born.
- The emerging paradigm of the Divine Feminine is led by paradox, with two seeming opposites simultaneously being true. With paradox, there is no right or wrong. The paradigm of the feminine is an embodied knowledge, meaning that we integrate our minds and bodies in the movement of our lives.
- When you begin to integrate your intuition and the wisdom of the body into your consciousness, it opens it up to the subtle multi-dimensionality of our entire existence and takes us out of *reacting* and instead opens us up to *allowing*.

Endnotes

1. Carl Jung, *The Earth Has a Soul: C.G Jung on Nature, Technology, and the Human Soul* (Berkeley: North Atlantic Books, 2002)
2. Clarissa Pinkola-Estes, *Women Who Run with the Wolves: Myths and Stories of the Wild Woman Archetype* (New York: Random House, 1992)

3

Shadow Swimming: Shedding Light on our Own Darkness

"The only way out, is through." ~Unknown

The shadow, whoooooohhoooo sounds scary, doesn't it? Throughout human history the shadow has been used in metaphors and stories to be the place where the scary things lurk and live. It's where darkness resides, and in a culture that is predicated on a religious foundation of living in the light - that being where God lives while the darkness is where Satan lives, it makes sense why we would be scared of it.

Even though I wasn't even raised religious I was still scared as shit of the Devil. Don't ask me where this fear came from, it seems I was just tapping into the collective energy of good and evil. I remember at night time, I made sure my mom left my door open and the hall light ON. If that shit wasn't on, I was gonna freak out. I had this fear that it was always in the darkness that the Devil was going to come and get me. The dark represented the time of the shadows, where bad things dwelled and the time when it was easier for them to come and get me as I wasn't able to see quite as clearly.

For years, I was so afraid of this evil force coming to *get me* that I would wait about an hour after my mom put me to bed and then ever so slowly tip toe into her room, sliding myself beside her. She would wake up almost every morning so irritated and wondering how the hell I got into her bed. I did this til I was 9, yes, 9. I was super tough as you can tell. The thing was though, that this fear was REAL. To me, the Devil represented a darkness of which I felt so deathly afraid. Where does a kid get this fear at 7 years old? I guess you hear enough stories of good and evil and you begin to believe them.

The light has nothing to find itself amidst or identify with if there is no darkness.

It has taken me years upon years to reframe what *the shadow* actually means to me. Our darkness or our shadow is essentially the parts of ourselves that we don't want to consciously identify with or for some reason are not able to consciously identify with– "consciously" meaning that it has reached the light of our conscious awareness, that part of us that is in waking time, able to see, process, and reflect on ourselves. And my aim here is to reframe this energy for you, so that we can take it out of this context of being *evil* and *bad* and begin to see it for what it is; deeper, hidden, unconscious aspects of ourselves that yearn to be expressed and seen.

For so many years we have equated "darkness" to "evil". But as the new paradigm of the feminine begins to emerge, it is time that we begin to integrate this darkness and allow it to be what it is; part of the light. For the light has nothing to find itself amidst or identify itself with if there is no darkness. We have been so trained to see these energies as separate when in fact they are unified— two parts of the same field. The dark and the light are one spectrum of one unified energy. In order for us to become truly whole and complete, we must begin to fully integrate and understand this so as to not shun and evade the darkness but to see it as an integral piece of ourselves; the place where the mystery lives, the gestation of life resides, and our deepest fears and desires hide themselves.

Journal Prompts

- Growing up, what was your individual relationship with-/view of the devil or evil? Did you have only dread or some curiosity?
- When did this view/relationship change into what it is today?

What Lives in the Dark?

One of the simplest ways to begin to understand the shadow is to begin to ask ourselves where in the entirety of our lives are we not able to be our true selves? This question can run long and deep and you may not even be able to answer it. Most likely because, from a very young age, you were shaped to be a certain way that negated the truth, the intuitive flowing part of you that just *was* and instead was replaced with a very strong *should be*. **Most of us have become so over identified with the *should be* that we have lost our own deep authentic truth**.

Because we have lived in a culture that is so based in keeping

69

up appearances, toxic appearances at that, it has forced us to put the aspects of ourselves that were not palatable to our families and friends somewhere else. The place we put this was in our shadow, the dark place, underground. The place inside. What people saw in the light was an image that was accepted, but what our truth was to us, was held inside, in the dark. And because we have been living in a dualistic paradigm up until now, to put them inside, in the dark, was to put them in the *bad* place. That place, in the darkness, has been so *bad* for so long that what ends up happening is that we put our *truth* in the *dark* so our truth ends up becoming bad.

For example, let's say as a kid you were in love with painting. The expression of color shook your soul and opened you to your authentic truth. There was no question that was what you wanted to pursue in your life. But you grew up in a family of all doctors and so choosing a life in the arts would be completely "selfish" and "irrelevant." Your family has a public image to uphold and a level of respect that the community has gathered from it. If you were to choose painting and not do well at it, you would be injuring the family name and image. So by the pressure of your mother and father, you decide to go into medicine. Something that you are not naturally good at but push yourself to pursue anyways instead of having to face the wrath of being an outsider who could be potentially poor and misunderstood by their entire family.

What ends up happening is that that part of you, the true painter, doesn't disappear, it goes underground deep inside of you, into the dark place. It's your truth, it's your essence and the feeling part of you that is guiding your life. It's the non-rational but authentic piece of your being that yearns to express itself. But because that isn't acceptable within the paradigm you grew up in, it goes down deep inside of you, and enters into the darker aspects of you. It's something that is inside of you, a truth that you and only you know is real and that you feel but that you are unable to express outwardly to the world. So there becomes a disconnect between the true you, and the you you show to the world.

You push your way through medical school, through all the academic rigors and hate it all the way through; your rational brain takes over your intuitive feeling self, and slowly you become more and more numb. But over time something begins to happen, you begin to see the reaction of people as you tell them you are a medical student. You see how they treat you and you begin to base your self worth on that praise. Over time the truth of yourself, the painter that yearns to express themselves through paint and color becomes lost and your life becomes more and more about the appearance of things-what is seen in 'the light'. People's opinions of you become more important than your own opinion of yourself, and you begin to garner the entirety of your worthiness from other people's perspective of yourself. As you begin to make more money, you become accustomed to the lifestyle you have created for yourself and become increasingly more and more numb to your truth. As the money grows, so does the disconnection from your own intuition, and in time, you have completely lost yourself, with every bit of material comfort known to man but holding onto a deep well of sadness and sorrow masked by an exterior of material pleasures and comforts. Over time, you end up barely being able to make a decision for yourself, questioning yourself to the deepest degree, and feeling frayed at all ends. This is because your soul is telling you one thing, but your mind is judging itself from the opinions of others. Your being becomes split, your shadow grows large, and the truth of your soul drowns in its own darkness.

In order for us to begin to increase the feminine power on this planet, we must first begin to honor the internal darkness in ourselves, the yin, feminine energy that is our truth. If we keep operating through "all systems as usual," we are perpetuating a sick system and are ourselves becoming numb, sick, and lost. It also keeps us all locked in a system where perpetual injustice is normalized. The "appearances" that we have kept have all been part of this patriarchy that is toxic. Recalibrating feminine energy on this planet means that we recalibrate it within ourselves first. That means beginning to excavate and honor the deep truths within ourselves that we have kept hidden to everyone and over time, even to ourselves.

Journaling Prompts

- What did you have to withhold in yourself as a child to be loved/accepted by your family?
- Did you suppress parts of yourself to be seen as okay?
- What parts of your authentic soul truth have you pushed underground to be accepted by society? What parts of your unique power have you hidden from others and yourself? How did you make yourself smaller, meeker?

Dismantling the Propensity of Othering

One of my teachers and colleagues, Toko-pa Turner, said it so well when she said that facing our shadow is when we begin to "Dismantle the propensity of othering[1]." What that means is that wherever in our lives we have been pointing the finger at someone, something, somewhere, saying, "YOU!...You are the reason for my unhappiness!" we begin to take that finger and turn it around to ourselves. Whoooweeeee is this hard work, and that is why I believe that anyone that dares to go this deep into themselves better be ready for what they are going to find, because there is a LOT of our own energy that we are putting onto so many things and people out there, unable to own our own shit.

Doing this work is the bravest work any human can do. I'm going to say that again, **beginning to bring the conscious light of awareness to the aspects of yourself you have never been able to see or wanted to face, is *the bravest work any human can do.*** We have been taught in our culture that a "warrior" is someone that puts themselves on the line and goes to war, facing their enemy in the name of fear, potentially dying, getting injured, or worse. This is one kind of warrior, sure. But the true warrior, the spiritual warrior, is one that goes into the darkest recesses of their own soul and psyche, the places where they have never dared to go because of the pain that lives there and chooses to sit with and open to those feelings and emotions. What is ironic is that this work is the bravest work yet those that are seen as being "brave" in our culture are those that subscribe to the macho warrior archetype and are generally too fearful to go to that place. They have been so trained out of their feelings, feeling their feelings and opening up to their own vulnerability that that would mean they were kind of shameful. This is what is so wrong with our culture and why we need to reframe the true power in opening to one's intuition and the feeling, feminine realm. This is the magical realm where hidden energies reside and until we begin to tap these energies within us, the world will remain the same. Revolution is upon us, and it is the internal revolution of the soul reckoning with itself. It is a deeply personal shadow revolution where the silent, etheric energies of this universe become highlighted, revered, and allowed out of their human imposed prison.

Revolution is upon us, and it is the internal revolution of the soul reckoning with itself.

I thought I had done every single thing one human could do to heal and become more whole. I worked with different teachers, went to various medicine ceremonies where I ingested plant medicine that took me to the darkest parts of my soul, I sat in stillness night upon night and prayed, offered, and asked Spirit to help me heal, help me learn how to love myself and become more worthy. It was these prayers I believe which led me to discovering the power of tapping my own shadow.

A few years ago, I was in the process of splitting with someone that I really believed was my soulmate. I was in the midst of a total and complete nervous breakdown and needed someone to talk to, not a shrink, but a Witch, a wise woman. I asked a friend of mine if she knew of anyone and she referred me to a woman who did shadow retrieval. This was the first I had heard of this kind of work and I was very intrigued. I went to this session and this woman put me on the table and asked me to come up with a situation with this person where I felt disgusted or upset. I immediately came up with a memory and started balling my eyes out, I was a wreck. Before I could get the words out, she asked me what was going on and I just could barely mutter from my own deep pit of grief, "He just hates himself so much."

I felt so sorry for this man, I was going into his pain and could now begin to feel it. At that moment as I felt so broken and so vulnerable, she responded to me with, "Do you hate yourself?" What a fucking question. Do I *hate* myself? Sheeesh. What kind of a question was THAT? Yet the thing was, that in that moment I didn't even have it in me to fight. The me of a month before that would have laughed and said, "No, I don't hate myself! Yes, I might have trouble loving myself at times, but I don't *hate* myself" had vanished and the raw, broken, and vulnerable as fuck me was laying on that table. There I was, on that table, finally stripped of all the levels of pride that held my identity intact, all the pride that had simultaneously kept me blocked from accessing the truth of my soul. In that moment, it had all vanished.

The me of a month prior had pride. A kind of pride that I was trained to have in this culture of pushing, striving, and keeping up appearances. It was my pride that kept my power intact. It was my pride that kept me feeling powerful. Pride is what we are taught as women to embody but it is also the very thing that keeps us from opening up to our pain. Pride keeps us powerful but it also keeps us locked in a kind of idea of how we want to *appear* instead of what we actually *feel*. In that moment, all of my pride had dissolved. I had been so cracked open and humbled by the pain of the relationship failing that I had no pride to keep up my appearance, and only the truth could come through. In that moment when she asked me, I was so raw and so cracked open by grief that it didn't take me very long to respond with a "yes." Yes, at that moment I did hate myself. Had I ever admitted this to myself? No.

This was the moment for me that changed everything. It was in that moment that my pride cracked open and I was able to let go of holding onto however it was that I wanted to appear to not just others, but to myself. **And this is the biggest piece**

when really diving into the world of the shadow, it's not just about how we want to appear to others, but it's how we want to appear to *ourselves*. What do I mean by this? It means that never in a million years would I want to identify as someone that hates herself, no-way Jose. I was a strong, Italian woman that had lived through a lot and came out the other side. I was powerful and brave, there is no way someone like the person I had become could *hate* themselves. Yet the truth was that up until that point, I had always lived in a darkness of my own that I never really saw as dark, it just simply was. Having a beauty queen/model mother and growing up in southern California pretty much set the stage for how I felt about myself for the rest of my life. Hours upon hours of nitpicking at my body and hair, feeling inadequate, feeling ugly. I would never have been able to admit to myself that I actually felt worthless, it was just something that I carried within me for so long, it was just part of my identity. But to outwardly admit that I felt worthless? I don't think so. That wasn't part of the story I was prepared to tell. I was in the midst of becoming "someone important"- an author and spiritual guide, and yet I hadn't ever been able to admit to myself that there were parts of myself that hated myself. I had an idea of who I wanted to be, and who I was becoming, how I wanted to *seem* to others. This didn't fit into my plan.

When I let this cat out of the bag, man oh man did my entire world change. For the first time in my entire life, I wasn't fighting myself anymore. I let go of the resistance. Being the Virgo that I am, I am acutely aware of myself and my thoughts. Up until that point I had noticed in my waking life when I was feeling like I didn't like myself, but because of all the new age training and reading I had done, I always fought this feeling.

I did NOT want to be someone that didn't like themselves, I wanted to be someone that loved themselves. So anytime I felt that feeling of dissatisfaction, unworthiness, hate, (which was a lot) I would curb it inside, and put on that happy face. I did not want to identify as someone that hates themselves because to me, that was weak. What this led to was me denying my truth, a truth that is dark and sad. And because I was so intensely denying it, it grew and grew, it became something I was always wrestling with, it became part of my identity.

When we hold ourselves to a standard that isn't our authentic truth, we end up fighting ourselves. We end up resisting the thing we so desperately don't want to identify with, ultimately attracting that energy to us.

That is what is funny about the shadow and holding ourselves to a standard that isn't our authentic truth, what ends up happening is that we end up fighting ourselves. We end up having so much resistance to the thing that we so desperately don't want to identify as that we innately end up attracting that energy to us. The old saying, "what you resist persists" is damn true in this context and it sucks.

I remember feeling so liberated after this. For the first time in my life, I was actually able to come to terms with my own imperfection and my god did that feel good. It was like a giant grey cloud had finally cleared and the truth of my being was set free. Upon letting this truth out, for the first time in my life I allowed myself to not just admit that I was imperfect, but to accept it. And this is what is so beautiful about shedding light on those parts of ourselves we have so desperately tried to hide for so long, because ultimately it comes down to wanting to *appear* a certain way, in essence, to be perfect. Sure, we may know logically that we aren't perfect, yet the standard that is set for us in this culture is so high and so unattainable that it's kind of our baseline programming. That is how our culture perpetuates itself, to set a standard for all of us that is in essence "perfect" which means, unattainable. This results in a chronic underlying self-loathing that we all carry within us, never able to quite fit the mark despite all the achievements and empowerment you have undergone.

I remember after having this revelation and beginning to allow myself the room to be "imperfect". I was in the bathroom looking in the mirror and I just admitted to myself, "There are parts of you that are ugly." This may seem rather extreme and dark, but actually, to my soul and the person I had been trying to be up until that point, it was one of the most liberating things I could have ever said to myself. I was, in essence, accepting my flaws. And not only accepting them but actively claiming them. Allowing parts of myself to be "ugly" meant that I gave myself permission and room to accept the things that I didn't like about myself. Instead of sitting in that constant state of resistance, a deep internal struggle to mask the things about myself that I didn't like, I just let them breathe, I let them be. God was this powerful.

Journaling Prompts

- Where has your pride kept you from accessing deeper, vulnerable truths about yourself?
- Where in your life is the disconnect between how you want to appear to others and how you actually feel about something/yourself?

- Getting past your pride is the key to accessing your shadow. What can you be gut-wrenchingly truthful about yourself? What have you not wanted to admit about yourself? Letting this OUT LIBERATES YOU and releases the resistance to the thing you most desperately do not want to be.

Where does your Shadow reveal itself?

Every one of us has our own shadow that can rear its head in its own way. I will never forget this story a client told me while we were talking about the shit that reallly triggers us, the stuff that just bugs the shit out of us, that being the road to our truth, wounding, and essentially, our freedom.

She told me the most hilarious story about her and her girlfriends that were at this very chic restaurant in New Mexico where every one of the servers looked like Jason Mamoa or Lenny Kravitz. The men were hot and the vibe was dope. They were all sitting around enjoying the atmosphere, laughing and drinking rosé when all of a sudden one of them spotted this woman and a man ferociously flirting with each other at a table near them.

The woman was sitting with her legs spread out and her foot up on the man's lap, where he was rubbing her dirty black feet that were taken out of her sandals. She was wearing a tank top, with no bra, had hairy armpits and BO (a part of me in the back of my head was like, uhhhm, have I ever been to Santa Fe? I was notoriously called "blackfoot" by my friends in college). This didn't sound all that nuts to me, but my client was fucking horrified. To take it even further she just KNEW those two were going to go home and fuck, and that the woman was going to be doing zero work. This woman had a most ostentatious kind of confidence which made my client seethe with frustration even further. She had not one iota of shame inside of her and the guy she was with was eating it up like sweet molasses.

My client had come from a Catholic-Mexican household where, as she puts, I was fed guilt and shame for every meal. To come face to face with a woman that was free and comfortable in her own body was angering her intensely. The thing was, it didn't just anger her, it angered the entire table of women with whom she was sitting. They all sat mouths open, watching this woman who was doing ZERO work meaning she wasn't *trying* at all, to have complete and total adoration from this man.

On the contrary these women waxed, shaved, and made every single move one can make before any man would ever touch them to make sure they were acceptable and "good enough." One of her friends said she wouldn't even let her boyfriend go down on her, which is sadly the case for so many women in America, genuinely ashamed of their bodies, consistently denying themselves pleasure for fear of how they may "appear."

This woman, with her hairy armpits, and laissez faire attitude was RIDICULOUS to my friend. To see a woman not trying at all, being her full female self and feeling PROUD of that? Oh no no no, that was too much for these women to compute, it was frying their circuit board. But this was the exact place where these women had the deepest level of unworthiness, where their deepest shame resided. This was their shadow, their darkness, the part they didn't consciously identify with and here it was coming directly up the surface, right smack dab in front of their faces. Here it was, the thing they hated most about themselves, the thing they feared the most, the thing that in the deepest place, the place they never fully admitted to themselves but instead did everything they could to *control* their ugliness, their pussy smell, their raw unadulterated femininity for fear of being "too much."

Witnessing someone with no shame, allowing themselves to be as they are in their body, was a mirror for these women. They saw right outside of themselves every single thing they felt shameful of in themselves. But because they had never fully admitted that to themselves, or allowed themselves to feel the pain and wounding that is beneath that deep need to control their environments, it came out as a hairpin trigger-seething, untamed, red hot *anger*. And this is how our shadow reveals itself when we still operate in a kind of denial about the parts of ourselves we don't want to identify with, or feel deep shame around.

The question is, how does your shadow reveal itself? What are the things that make your blood boil with resentment, anger, or a deep bitterness? Where in your life are you still held behind a shroud of darkness? And are you willing to have the courage to find out what it is all *really* about? Because I will tell you, if you are, this is the work that will truly transform your life.

The first step in beginning to find your truth and power is to begin to bring conscious awareness to the places in our lives we get *triggered* meaning, the places that truly make us kind of lose our shit. Instead of moving forward with our normal hair-pin reactions to things, we stop, take a second, and allow ourselves to access what is underneath that emotion. We begin to breathe, stop, and inquire. The reason why this is such a profound moment is that what we are ultimately doing is taking responsibility for ourselves, our pain, and our emotions. This doesn't deny the truth, for instance, if we were abused or bullied or had some horrible childhood that is keeping us locked in a

81

kind of insecurity, anger, and victimhood that moves into our adult life. **What this moment of recognition does is begin to say to ourselves, our abusers, and to the Universe that we are ready to take our power back, and that no thing and no one, no matter how evil or bad can take our joy or power in the present.**

Journaling Prompts:

- Where does your shadow reveal itself?
- What are the things that make your blood boil with resentment, anger, or a deep bitterness?
- Where in your life are you stuck in anger/resentment- can you tap the grief behind it? And even further, its origin?
- Who are you most jealous of? Can you reconcile with these qualities you are not fully being able to embody in yourself?

Triggers

The truth is that the shadow is where our fullest potential and ultimate power resides. And chances are if you are reading this book, that is what you freaking want. It's what I so desperately wanted, and that's why I'm writing this book, so that you can have it too. One can only go on for so many years absolutely hating themselves, never feeling like they are enough, and giving society at large all their power. Not only that, but for us to be in tune with our deepest power, strength, and purpose, we gots to know ourselves through and through. And we will never ever know ourselves, *really* know who we are if we do not begin to play around in our own darkness. If we don't explore this work, there will always be a part of us that we are ignoring, because we are scared of it, even subconsciously- and that part is the part that feels unworthy and shameful. Paradoxically, when one holds the power of opening to our shadow we are opening up to our greatest joy as well because there is nothing holding us back or blocking our energy.

Paradoxically, when we open up to our shadow, we open up to our greatest joy.

The saying, "the only way out is through" was written about this very topic. There is no way out of this work other than moving through it. The key to moving through it is to begin to identify when you feel "triggered" which is a word that is being very overused these days but in this case, it basically means when someone or something is making you internally lose your shit. What that means, is that you have to start getting realllly honest with yourself about the stuff that bothers you. This is how you really get to know yourself and who you really are. I think so many of us walk around in a perpetual state of annoyance or anger, but because it's so constant, we just see it as our M/O and don't really question it. I know I did, and still do sometimes, I am by no means perfect.

Beginning to do shadow inquiry is beginning to notice when people, places, things etc. start to make you lose your shit in some way or another. And yes, there are varying degrees of this, of course. There are slight annoyances, like the guy at my local Whole Foods who is always super friendly to me and I think may even have a crush on me but who annoys the fuck out of me for some goddamn reason. The old me would have just stopped there, kept up my annoyance and kept myself feeling superior in some way. Because this is also what the shadow does, when something or someone annoys us and we don't question it, it automatically makes us superior to them or better than them. This is the linear paradigm of hierarchy that I was talking about earlier just playing itself out to a tee.

So instead of ignoring this man, the me of today chooses to engage further with him. I'm not Mother Teresa and some days when I'm in a mood, I do ignore him. But on most days, I go in there and face my discomfort with him, pay attention to myself throughout the entire exchange and begin to ask myself, "What is it in him that I dislike in myself?" Or even deeper, "Does he have some quality that I have been unable to adopt in myself for whatever reason?" Like I said, some days I'm just in a shitty mood and don't have the bandwidth to do that kind of self-inquiry but most days, I go in there and face him, through all the discomfort. I've become more curious than afraid, and that is the tipping point with this work. It's when we desire to be free in the deepest sense of the word, to know ourselves, and to embrace joy more often than we do fear. I'm more curious to understand my true nature, and to understand why I react the way I do, seeing that the truth is that underneath that reaction is a kind of endless suffering, whether it be through anger, spite, unworthiness, all masked behind a kind of superiority. I'm more curious to find out what is underneath there now than I am to keep up that level of limited consciousness.

I've become more curious than afraid, and that is the tipping point with this work.

A higher level of being triggered would be watching a rape scene in a movie when you yourself had been raped. There

84

is definitely a spectrum of what it means to be internally losing your shit or "triggered" but the most important thing is that we begin to notice ourselves. Instead of just going on auto-pilot as we have been doing for years, we begin to wake up to our emotions, honor them, and begin to witness them. This is us witnessing the divine feminine within ourselves, the part of us that empathizes and witnesses pain. It's beginning to give it space and room, to allow it to be, and to honor it for the powerful force that it is.

There is a big trend these days about being "triggered" and forcing everyone around you to bow to your emotions, walk on eggshells, and coddle you. That is not the kind of "triggering" I am talking about here. Unfortunately, many people use this energy to get attention, and to manipulate others. That is the energy of the dark feminine rearing its head. Coming to this work with an open heart and desire to uncover the truth of your own soul will innately trigger you; the point is to learn how to internally handle it so that it doesn't become the problem of those around you. When it becomes the problem of others around you, you are projecting your pain onto others, and not owning your own story. Being triggered is an internal process. It is something that happens inside of us and us alone. Its ok to need support during this process, if it is genuine. What I have noticed in our culture is that most people don't feel they can handle the emotions that comes with being triggered and they project it outwards. This is the crux of this issue of being triggered, it's examining how we actually feel about ourselves and whether or not we feel we can handle our own emotions.

What do I mean by "handle?" I mean process, own, and transmute the energies on our own. Because when we own this energy completely, and work with it individually, we then take

ALL of our power back into ourselves. Sure, we all need guides, and facilitators- as I am to you right now. But when entering this work, be wary- a true guide will lead you back to yourself. All others desire a relationship where you *need* them to heal. I have learned this through being a healer myself and going to countless healers, the best in the world- throughout my travels. We are all our own greatest spiritual teacher, and all of the healing medicine we need is right inside of us. Marlon Brando is quoted as saying that he had over 30 years of psychotherapy, and in that time it did absolutely nothing for him. It wasn't until he brought the mirror to his own face and did the inner work to truly face himself, was there a deep kind of transmutation that happened.

Once you begin to notice what is making you subtly or overtly lose your shit by getting triggered either externally or internally— or both, you can begin to notice the resistance that you hold within yourself. This is really the crux of what the shadow is allll about y'all. Because of all of our cultural conditioning of *good* and *bad*, our culture has placed these darker emotions that we may be experiencing as *bad* and therefore we keep ourselves in a state of resistance to those emotions. What this means is that we resist having them, we resist their existence, we resist ourselves, all of it. For so long, emotions, the darkness, our truth, all of it that makes up our deep internal world and that which is essentially the realm of the feminine, has been seen as weak, irrational, and bad. That means we do NOT want to be having them. So we resist them. We dismiss them and we do everything we can to destroy them. It's the resistance to them that intensifies them and makes them all even bigger. What ends up happening is we have chronic depression, chronic anxiety, or we get sick in some way.

Whatever our truth is, no matter how swallowed and stuffed down it has gone, it can never be destroyed. And over time, if it is never given agency, power, and voice it will be the thing that will eventually destroy us. That is when a true darkness will emerge, and because of our own numbness and hidden shame we will project this darkness onto others, gaining pleasure in excess, greed, and pain. Opening to our shadow, gives us space to allow this darkness out of the closet, so that it can breathe and be seen.

We have been coronated into the era of the Divine Feminine and this is an era of emotion. Our truest and deepest emotions, the ones that we ourselves don't fully understand how to even wrestle with, are in the shadow. It's only feared and seen as bad because it isn't able to be understood. When we begin to take the cultural "charge" off of it and off of the fear of it, we begin to reconcile that part of us that has been so desperate to be felt.

Releasing resistance essentially, is opening up to the thing we have so desperately been running away from and avoiding at all costs. When you open to the thing you have seen as separate, you integrate that energy into yourself. *This* is the most powerful and potent work. This is the alchemical moment that makes for a true expansion of consciousness and creates transformation. **Releasing resistance means that whatever the hell you have not been wanting to feel– you surrender to, and fucking feel. This is the moment y'all. This is it. This is the moment of true courage, that only you and your inner self will ever know**. It was just too much, too painful, too intense, too whatever for you to really look at, it's the moment that you say, "I'm not your servant, I'm not your victim, I'm not your whore anymore." And you turn and face it. The fear is what keeps us enslaved, the fear is what keeps us small. When we turn to face the thing we have so desperately not wanted to face, we rise up into the powerful Witches that we are. In the moment that we turn and face the thing that has had power over us for eons we not only take our power back but we *become* the power. This is the moment where we rise from the ashes and become the fucking Phoenix's that we are. This is the alchemy of transformation.

Workbook Questions to Journal

· I want you to work with this shadow inquiry method:

-**Triggers;** Identify the trigger that sets you off onto an anger/resentment spiral. Is there a consistent theme? Begin to honestly notice your patterns.

-**Resistance;** Notice how you feel about this thing, and the resistance you are holding to whatever emotion is underneath the anger. Notice the excuses you make to yourself to keep yourself from actually facing the deeper truth of the issue. This is a tough step, because it forces us to dissolve our ego, so that we may actually get to the heart of the wounding.

-**Integration;** Instead of remaining in a pattern of anger that tethers us to a reactive loop, we inquire and ask ourselves, "What is this really about?" After we ask ourselves this, we are truly able to integrate the truth behind the emotion. This is the alchemical moment when we stop projecting our energy outwards and own our own story, wounding, and truth. This is when our true power emerges.

-**Transparency;** When we are honest with ourselves about what we are actually feeling, we become transparent, meaning we are not hiding a deeper truth. When we are transparent, we hold a deep level of self-respect and those around us sense a deeper integrity that we hold. We don't feel the need to wear such a thick mask anymore, and are more comfortable sharing ourselves with humility.

Altar Power

We cannot do this work alone y'all so this is why we have the established altar space that we sit at and pray . This is all work that is of Spirit, and in order to go that deep, we must access the power and wisdom of infinite love itself. When you first start doing this work, pay attention to the things that trigger you. From there, begin to open up to the truth of what is behind the trigger. The emotional responses that ensue can become kind of inconvenient. What you are essentially doing, is giving yourself permission to *feel*. This may seem like a small thing, but in a culture that is based in control, releasing these emotions is a wild and rebellious act. Giving yourself permission to feel, is the deepest honor you could ever give yourself. What you are finally doing, maybe for the first time in your life, is witnessing your pain, which means that you are allowing yourself to be seen, but by no one but you and God.

We think that hiding our pain is what makes us strong, but it's actually the thing that diminishes our self-worth. Because essentially, we feel ashamed of our pain, we feel ashamed of having any pain at all. Within the PWC, we have been trained to feel ashamed of our pain and so we have de-sensitized ourselves and become numb to the natural world, ourselves as part of it. That's why our feelings have become so dark and distorted, and been stuffed so deep down. Whatever "identity" one constructs while carrying this darkness within them, never fully being seen or felt, is exactly that, an "identity." It is something designed to please others. There may be elements of the truth inside that filter out into that identity, but as long as we have that piece inside that is still hidden, we will never be able to fully spread our wings and fly. There will always be something that we are protecting, using our energy for, something that we are scared to show others. **It's so ironic because so much of history has been so trained to be afraid of the shadow —where the dark things lurk and live, but the shadow itself isn't what is dark, the shadow just holds our truth, something we keep underground. The true darkness is the resistance to our truth. The darkness is knowing that we have something, a truth, a feeling, a sadness, and keeping it hidden.**

Meditative Journeying Exercise

Use this process when you feel triggered by any external situation and feel yourself blindly reacting, i.e., anger, spite, judgment, etc. Instead of moving forward with that emotion, take a moment and pause, breathe, and ask yourself the deeper question, "What is this all really about?" Sit with that emotion, try and expand it, and feel if you can connect it to another time in your life that you felt that same emotion. Try and connect it to a memory if you can. Often this may mean that if you are in a public place, you'll need to excuse yourself to go and sit with your true emotions privately. This usually boils down to a core wound, and that wound, as we begin to access and process it, begs to be witnessed and felt. This requires feeling your feelings completely and allowing yourself to grieve for your own soul and younger self if need be.

Getting to the root of the issues opens us up to our authentic selves. It begins to shine the light of conscious awareness on the darkest aspects of ourselves, meaning the parts we are not even fully aware of/don't want to fully identify with. This is the most powerful work any human can do and is what will transform you on a path to true awakening. Try this step-by-step process to uncover your core wounding. This process was partially inspired by the work of Holistic Mental Health Coach, Catherine Liggett:

1. Sit comfortably at your altar. Light a candle and breathe deeply from the base of your spine to the crown of your head. Breathe slow and deep, do it five times.
2. Invoke the protection and guidance from your ancestors and guides. Ask them to come and be present with you while you move through this process. If at any time any piece of this journey becomes difficult, call on their strength to assist you through it.
3. Think about a recent memory that triggered you massively; it can be anything large or small, just something that really fucking bothered you. Just use whatever comes up.
4. Once you come up with that situation, I start to identify the feelings surrounding this. What is it? Anger? Sadness? Numbness? If you were uncomfortable, take a deep breath and go INTO that feeling and identify it.
5. Now breathe into that feeling to intensify and expand them. Feel it expanding and leaving the confines of your physical body with each breath. Breathe in and out of your mouth, scooping into your belly, opening more and more to the discomfort. It is this discomfort that begs to be seen. It is the part of ourselves that is yearning to be witnessed and honored for their pain. This is bringing conscious awareness to the darkness inside. You are a warrior.

6. Can you find words to describe what this feeling is? This is the core feeling.

7. Go deeper into your consciousness and identify another time with this same or similar core feeling. Move into the memory, and allow yourself to fully embody that setting again. Allow the new flavor of this core feeling to rise, expand even further, and enter the feeling deeper and deeper. Is there anything else that is seen or heard about this feeling? Be curious. Does it have a color? Place in the body?

8. Freeze this scene. Imagine the strongest version of your-self as an adult visiting your younger self in this scene. You may, at this point, look at their in the eyes. What do you see?

9. Now invoke the power of the Divine. Ask that higher power to bless, witness, and bow to this young child who was put in this situation. Let them know you see them, witness them, and honor them for who they are. Using the force of love you carry with you, you validate, honor, and love this young child. You see them for who they are, not what others wanted them to be, and you stay in that scene as long as it feels right for you. You may say or do anything that feels right until they feel right.

10. From there, you can thank your guides and Spirit for assisting you through that process.

After using this practice, journal what you discovered and found, and give yourself time to process and rest, this is deep work, and it will take time to integrate into your body and life.

WITCHY BITCH WISDOM

- Our darkness or our shadow is essentially the parts of ourselves that we don't want to or are unable to consciously identify.
- Recalibrating feminine energy means that we recalibrate it within ourselves first, beginning to excavate and honor the deep truths that we have kept hidden to everyone, even ourselves.
- "Dismantling the propensity of othering" means that wherever in our lives we have been pointing the finger at someone, something, somewhere, saying, "YOU!...You are the reason for my unhappiness!" – instead we begin to take that finger and turn it around to ourselves.
- Shedding light on those parts of ourselves we desperately tried to hide frees us from needing to 'appear' a certain way, in essence, to be perfect. Being perfect, which is perpetuated by our culture, is unattainable and results in a chronic underlying self-loathing that we carry within us, never able to hit the mark despite our achievements.
- The first step in beginning to find your truth and power is to begin to bring conscious awareness to the places in our lives we get 'triggered' meaning, the places that truly make us kind of lose our shit. Instead of moving forward with our normal hair-pin reactions to things, we instead stop, take a second, and allow ourselves to access what is underneath that emotion.
- Because of all of our cultural conditioning of 'good' and 'bad', our culture has placed these darker emotions that we may be experiencing as 'bad' and therefore we keep ourselves in a state of resistance to those emotions.

- Give yourself permission to feel. This may seem like a small thing, but in a culture that is based in control, releasing these emotions is a wild and rebellious act. Giving yourself permission to feel, is the deepest honor you could ever give yourself.
- The true darkness is the resistance to our truth. The darkness is knowing that we have something, a truth, a feeling, a sadness, and keeping it hidden.
- The true darkness is the resistance to our truth. The darkness is knowing that we have something, a truth, a feeling, a sadness, and keeping it hidden.

Endnotes

1. Toko-pa Turner, *Belonging: Remembering Ourselves Home* (Vancouver: Her Own Room Press, 2018)

4

Wild Authenticity: Rewilding the Self Home

"Allow yourself to be silently drawn by the strange pull of what you truly desire and it will not lead you astray."
~Rumi

Rewilding. I freaking love this word. It speaks to something primordial within every one of us and it grants us the permission and freedom to reclaim that truth. My entire life I have been endlessly searching for that wildness, literally going to the edges of the earth to rekindle that thing that I was so desperate to reignite inside of me. Something that I felt I was always missing, a kind of freedom.

I've always described myself as a "seeker," someone that was endlessly searching for the truth. I had no idea what it was or where it was, but I wanted to find it. All I knew was where the wildness wasn't. It wasn't in the shopping malls filled with photographs of airbrushed and emaciated models. It wasn't in the supermarkets with every packaged + processed food I could ever desire at my fingertips. It wasn't in the bars or the late-night hookups, half-conscious and unable to feel much. It wasn't at the office job, locked in a prison of machines with all basic human urge and instinct quelled, numbed, and subdued. There was a wildness for which I ached , something that was not packaged or planned. Something that no human had ever touched and tampered with, something raw. Yet it seemed that the more I searched, the more it eluded me.

By the end of college, I was desperate for something wild. My wild soul had just endured 20 years of institutionalized "education." Some people find their *out* at school, they get lost in the knowledge and find freedom in it. Not me. English and Art were always my favorite topics and the ones in which I excelled; early on I realized how to just go through the motions and make it through so that I wouldn't be bothered. I always did the work as I was instructed to do but never put any real effort into it. I just did what I was supposed to do, always waiting and waiting for the day I could be left to my own devices, liberated. I wasn't into the competition mentality, always striving and seeking for that one space at the top. I always felt I was in some sort of cage, it may not have had metal bars, but it was there. I was always waiting for the day that I could choose what direction I wanted to go in, who I wanted to become, and where I wanted to put my energy. By the time junior high rolled around, I was already way *over* school. I wanted to be outside, engaging with life. As the years rolled on and my consciousness grew, I felt like I was in a kind of prison. Waking up, dressing, and trudging along to school to regurgitate what was asked of me. There was no creativity, no spark, no joie de vivre.

I was so desperate to take time off after high school, to catch my breath and breathe- figure out who I was outside of every institution. I was desperate to rekindle my wildness, to find my own voice and vision. My mom would not allow it though. She was so afraid that I would not ever go back to school that she pushed me to go to college straight from high school.

And there I went, the general melancholia and malaise that had been the truth of my life endlessly continuing. I am very aware that I sound like a very privileged white American complaining about my "education," but this was a very real pain. Yes, I had opportunity and a certain kind of freedom but my entire life I was put in institution after institution that I didn't want to be in, and which I felt dead inside of. My intuitive, feminine, Witchy soul was so diminished, so unseen. There was no place for the mystery, the psychic realm, there was no place for magic. I craved the natural world and the realm of Spirit, yet because it had never been offered as any option, I went along with what was expected of me, always uncertain of what I was missing but feeling a continuous emptiness, a lingering void that never felt fulfilled.

And this is an essential piece most don't acknowledge when discussing "education." Our entire institutionalized education system is built by the same thread of consciousness that colonized this land on which we now reside. That thread is a white, male, ruling order. But even deeper, it is based on a fundamental imbalanced patriarchal system that values rationality over intuition. It is imbalanced and therefore has become dis-eased. It is hard to pinpoint how an entire system can be so imbalanced, or how something that has been so normalized over millennia could be so fundamentally flawed. But the truth is that because of the Patriarchal WORLD Culture, our entire world is predicated on this truth. And it is what has been pushed down our throats from the time we can walk and talk. We are taught to reason, and that reason itself is the paramount form of intelligence from the time we are babies. **Because the Divine Feminine was systematically eliminated, any culture, or way of life that didn't value rationality as its benchmark for intelligence was seen as carnal, stupid, savage, and just plain dumb**.

I suppose that is why there is a part of me that has a deep found resentment of English culture, the epitome of "refinement." What is this refinement but the death of all feeling, intuition, magic, and Spirit? This false idealization of class is still upheld here in the USA. Because class is based on hierarchy, one over the other, one better than the other, we hold that as a standard. Hierarchy was bred out of patriarchy, the idea that something, someone, is always better and more worthy. And that essentially, there is one thing at the top that is the ideal. This is the deep, silent, and ingrained thinking that has been carved into us from birth. It's the American ideal. But it's not even in America, it's all over the world. Hierarchy and class are how power and control are maintained and dominated. And that exists everywhere...from the caste system in India, a spiritual system that justifies your worthiness based on Karma to classes all over the world. This is how our reality has been organized for eons. Well, I write this here and now to say, "Not no mo'." **We have entered a new era, the era of the Divine Feminine, and this is an era of collectivism and collaboration**. This is an era of paradox. For the first time in eons as we Witches come out of the closet, we are giving ourselves permission to express our wildly authentic selves. As we come out of the closet and remember our truth and power, we are simultaneously midwife-ING this new era. One of collaboration, unity, and feminine power.

For so many years, I was seeking the wild; going from Morocco to Hawaii, from China all the way to the Alaskan wilderness. In 2012, I was working on a biodynamic farm in Maui, HI. Biodynamic farming is very Witchy. It is a type of farming invented by Rudolph Steiner and it includes using herbs and crystals and tracking the movement of the planets in relation to planting and harvesting cycles. Having grown up in front of the television day after day eating packaged cereal and quoting the Golden Girls, being this in tune with the earth was the most wild and free I had ever been. Every day I was directly interacting with the soil, I had my hands in the earth and was dirty as fuck. I loved it. They called me Messy Jessie as a kid, and nothing made me happier than to be digging ditches and playing around in the dirt. I remember one day while I was planting seeds into the earth, I was squatting and placing 3 tiny seeds into a small hole a ½ inch into the soil. The sun was shining through the clouds. All was silent except for the wind rustling through the palm trees. A light breeze touched my cheek as I looked up into the sky and it was in that solitary moment that I felt the happiest I have ever felt in my life.

Simultaneously, it was at that moment that I realized that women and the earth were one. A woman's womb was akin to that of the earth. Seeds get planted and the earth nourishes and gestates the life of the seed as it grows into a full plant. This process is parallel to the growth of the human within the female womb. I had the profound realization that the disregard and destruction of the natural world was aligned with the destruction of the divine feminine, and it was at that moment that I vowed to do something about it. I didn't know what I was going to do, but I was going to do something.

So there I went, finding a master's degree program in Sustainable Communities. I discovered the discipline of Ecofeminism, a branch of study that merged feminism and ecology. I felt like I was onto something, and was inspired and motivated to affect change. As I began graduate school I felt awake and optimistic. That optimism soon turned into exhaustion, depletion, and an overall sense of unworthiness as I was placed smack dab right back in the center of our mainstream educational system. This program had advertised itself as a revolutionary program and there was nothing else like it out there. It showed students engaged in real community projects, things that were hands-on. Yet by the time I had gotten myself knee-deep in the program, it wasn't what I had been expecting. This program was alternative and radical, yes, but it was still inside of the old educational paradigm. We were still day in and day out in classrooms with 4 walls. We were talking and reading and talking and reading. Arguing and every one of us feeling insecure, discriminated against, and desperate to get our voices heard. The competition was outrageous, and the level of activism was like nothing I'd ever experienced, fueled by a never-ending pit of rage and anger, of injustice against "the system."

It was in that program that I actually read from Audre Lorde, one of the great American black lesbian feminists. This quote seemed to be the cornerstone of my entire experience in grad-uate school, a quote I could never quite shake. A quote that kept me up at night. She said, "The master's tools will never dismantle the master's house.[1]" What this means essentially is that you cannot use the same kind of "tools" i.e, thinking, logic, consciousness- to dismantle and change the "house" or system which created it. Yet here we were, in this grandiose institution, behind 4 walls doing exactly that, using the master's tools to try and tear down that motherfucking house.

100

It wasn't until I took a class with one woman, Dr. Janine Schipper, that my experience in graduate school began to change. Janine was very different than the rest of the professors. This woman was a Buddhist but also carried this otherworldly sense about her. She was ferociously intuitive and didn't hide that fact. She organized her classes in a very egalitarian manner and had almost no ego, sitting humbly as a student herself during many of the seminars, acknowledging how much she herself was learning from her students. This was in stark contrast to the male academic egos that I had been absorbing that gave off the sense that you must compete, dominate, and work your ass off to be the best. Those classes were filled with a constant undercurrent of shame, all of us scrounging and scraping to *win*.

Dr. Schipper's class was very different, it was quieter, more intuitive, more contemplative. We meditated and went into other realms. She challenged us to explore different kinds of consciousness and it was in her class, *Consciousness and Social Change* that I, for the first time in my entire schooling, felt seen.

At the time, I didn't have the language for it, but all I knew was that I resonated deeply with her and needed to follow whatever she was passing out. Now in 2019, after taking my own Witchy self out of the closet, I understand that she is a Witch, a wise woman deeply in tune with nature and other realms of consciousness in service of healing. And she somehow managed to find a way to offer her magic within the system. She is one of those amazing humans that can master both the rational/intellectual and the intuitive/feeling. She continues to be a dear friend and mentor to me.

When I came across Janine's class, I was at the edge of my rope. Feeling increasingly stifled, restricted, unseen, and once again forced into a certain kind of knowledge that wasn't my natural flow. I was exhausted and unsure if I should even continue in the program. I love the quote, "If you judge a fish by its ability to climb a tree, it will live its whole life believing it's stupid$_2$." Well, I was always that fish always trying to climb that tree. I was parched, exhausted, and desperate to swim in the depths. When I came across Janine, I felt like I had finally found the ocean after a lifetime of swimming in a muddy puddle in the middle of a gigantic redwood forest.

Immediately I made her my thesis chair, and together we explored a thesis topic. Janine saw me, and was the one that came to me with the phrase, *rewilding*. I took to it like hot coals on a fire. This was where the true work between Janine and I began. Even though Janine was an undercover Witch, finding her own covert ways of bringing the intuitive, feeling, and magic to academia, she was still a classically trained tenured professor. No one had ever seen HER as the Witch that she was, so how could she fully acknowledge it in me?

So when I came to her with thesis ideas, she threw piles of books at me on topics that would take me eons to sift through. Interesting ideas but very heady and dense. This felt so narrow, so rigid. So. Boring. I needed MORE, I needed more dimensionality, and to bring in other kinds of consciousness. I trusted and loved her though, and did not fully know how to express this to her, all I knew was that this classic way was killing my soul and putting me in a box I'd so desperately been trying to find my way out of my entire life.

I didn't realize it at the time but now am able to see that this was a very old and deep wound on which we were hitting. This was the wound I had carried since birth perpetually and forever dismissing my truth and power because no one could ever see it or deem it worthy. I had so much pain I was holding, so much wisdom and healing energy that I was ready to offer the world yet here I was again, getting asked to shove all of that power into a very rigid and narrow box in order to be seen as "legitimate." This is the perpetual wound of the Witch. Up until this point in time, there has been no place or space for us Witches to express our power. It has resulted in us dismissing ourselves, our needs, our truth, our voice, and our innate worth to this planet. I didn't have the words for this then, all I knew was that to have her, my only confidant at this rational institution put me in another box, was heartbreaking.

One day I came to her office when we were to have a discussion on my topic. I sat in the chair in her office and couldn't hold back the tears. I just started balling and did my best to try and explain to her how narrow and confining this felt, how horribly rigid and boring. I didn't know that I was crying out from the depths of the deepest feminine wound. The wound of our power and wisdom, our intuition and emotion going unseen, once again. I was crying for every woman and man that had never been seen for who they were. My soul couldn't do it. She sat with me, looked me in the eyes, and felt my pain. What was different about Janine was that because she didn't have the ego and natural hierarchy of the other professors, she naturally collaborated with you. She would give you what most humans in this world cannot give anyone, her complete and utter attention. She witnessed me, and in that, opened herself up to being transformed. This is truly the divine feminine incarnate. Our exchange was the first I had with a professor that was supposedly "above me" therefore "better" than me, who chose to collaborate and collectivize with me. In all my other classes, I was studying collaborative economies and alternative methods of living but nowhere was it actually and honestly being modeled to me. It was only there, in her office, that she gave me what no one had ever given me, transformative attention.

What I ended up doing was a thesis based on rewilding consciousness. It was the seed of what you are reading now. Nevertheless, as graduate school ended, I was utterly exhausted. When my acupuncturist took my pulse, she could barely find it. Janine was my ocean of refuge, but I was still forced to engage in a lot of mainstream academia that was so rigid and linear that by the time it was over, I had nothing left. I had been studying rewilding for a few years by then, yet I felt so far away from anything truly wild. I craved deeply to be immersed in nature and to lose myself inside of its womb. Here I was at the end of my rope, having just completed one of the hardest things I had ever endured, and now where would I go? I was lost and uncertain and I craved absolute freedom. I didn't know what it looked like but I felt deep in my heart I needed something really wild.

Journal Prompts

- Can you relate to this story? If so, where in your life has your spirit gone unseen?
- What has your experience been in the world of "education?" What kind of education have you received and has it truly honored your gifts?
- Can you see how institutional education can dominate our natural power and consciousness? Has it for you?

Fear of the Wild

When my ex-boyfriend Luke, offered me the opportunity to come up to Anchorage, Alaska to live with him, I chose to go. Getting back together with an ex, what a great idea. Going to a place that is dark, cold, and very far away from all family and friends, what an even better idea! And on top of it, I had none of my own independent income yet and little savings. I was seriously setting myself up for major success, doh!

At that point I so desperately wanted to be in a relationship, I was so, so tired of going at it alone and making my way in this imbalanced masculinized world. So there I went, putting ALL of my eggs in one very rickety, unraveling basket.

At this point, I was in my spiritual flow, praying and sitting at my altar but I had not yet been fully awakened to what it meant to live as the Witch that I was. I still had a lot of fear and didn't understand how to open myself up to trusting in the universe fully. Even deeper, I didn't fully trust my intuition nor did I fully trust Spirit working through me. I still doubted myself and the Divine. Still though, born naturally in tune, there was this feeling inside of me that somehow knew that I was lying to myself. I made up story after story, rationalizing the HELL out of why this was a good idea. There were many "reasons" why this was a good idea, but underneath all those reasons was a feeling that I couldn't evade. The feeling just KNEW this was the wrong move.

Isn't this the story of all of us Witches? Underneath all the reasoning and logistics we KNOW what to do, but because the culture at large doesn't honor intuition or simply making choices based on a "feeling," we go with the rational, reasoned, and analyzed approach. This culture at large directly trains us OUT of our intuition. It teaches us to not trust what we feel, and therefore we don't trust what we feel. We don't trust ourselves. When one doesn't trust themselves, they innately feel unworthy because they are unable to access their truth. This is a very profoundly important part of reclaiming one's self-worth and something that no one has ever really taught us Witches. This is precisely why our culture has become so numb. We have been trained for millennia upon millennia that our natural feelings are wrong. True worth comes from knowing yourself through and through and acting in accordance with that. Having been trained out of our truth, we cannot access our true potential and self-worth. We second guess ourselves, and stuff whatever truth we are feeling down our throats because it isn't convenient, and doesn't fit in correctly.

This voice, this feeling that we have been trained out of honestly feeling IS our wildness. The wildness is the natural flow-state. And it is the thing that we are so desperate to reclaim. The thing we can't put our finger on as to what exactly is missing, but simply having a feeling there is something not quite right. It is the natural part of ourselves, the piece that *is* Spirit. As we begin to open ourselves up further and further to living alongside this force of Love, we begin to acknowledge that this force lives inside of us and is the purest thing that can never be fully seen or measured. It is only something that can be felt. Spirit, the guiding energy of universal consciousness is wildness at its core. It is what gives birds flight, it's what makes leaves green, it's what creates the crimson color of the setting sun. This ethereal, enigmatic power– this raw untouched purity *is* spirit, and it *is* the Wild force that makes the color of our blood red, and the sight behind our eyes clear. We are this force, and this wildness can never be taken from us, only forgotten.

I went to the edges of the earth seeking this wildness, all the way to the wildest of places, Alaska. After leaving Luke, I finally got my own cabin in the woods. This was what I thought my dream was. I was about 45 minutes outside of town along a dirt road. I felt like a badass, living out in the wild, raw, untouched Alaskan wilderness. The thing was, it really was wild out there. On any given day I was surrounded by wolves, coyotes, bears, eagles, and moose. I would go on walks with my dog (a little guy only 16 lbs) and feel deep waves of fear that he could get snatched up. One day, as I was walking through the woods and my dog Nico caught a scent and ran into the woods chasing after an entire grouping of gigantic 400 lb moose. I lost my shit. Moose were notorious for being even more deadly than bears, especially if they had babies with them. I screamed for Nico and couldn't find him anywhere. All I heard was rustling and movement deep in the dense-ass forest. He had disappeared for a good 15 minutes, me calling after him, freaking out that he had died. Finally, he came running out of the woods, crap all over him. I almost completely lost it.

Here I was, finally living in the wildest way I could ever live, surrounded by raw, untouched landscape and I was scared shitless. I sat back on my porch and stared at the pristine snow-capped mountains, breathed them in, and then tilted my head towards the sky asking myself, "What in the hell are you really looking for out here?" I couldn't help asking myself if this was the way that I truly wanted to live. I was searching for the wild, wanting so badly to be immersed in a purity untouched by human doing yet there I was, more trapped and helpless than I could ever imagine, encased in a fear I couldn't even begin to name. What I realize now, was that I was running away from my own inner wildness and at my own core afraid of facing myself and my own power. I had been running for years—running away from myself or running towards myself, it's hard to say. I was in a constant search, seeking it outside of myself the only thing that could only be found within.

And so the true journey of reconciling what "wildness" really was became evident to me. **The truth was that wildness was not anything outside of myself, it was not a kind of raw, untouched earthly purity that would somehow wash my soul clean of all its fear, judgment, anger, hatred, and greed. I was seeking outside of myself the very thing I was unable to tap within. The wildness was, after all not a thing. It was an energy.** And that energy lived inside of the untouched nature I was forever chasing just as it lived in the dirty pigeons that lined the streets of New York City, just as it lived in me. What up until that point I had been unable to see was that the wild was always there, just waiting to be witnessed.

I had gone to literally the edges of the earth, deep into the darkness, to find something pure, something untouched. But the fundamental piece I was blind to was that I believed this *thing* was separate from me. **What I understand now, is that the wildness I was so desperate to find, was really the Witch within, begging to be seen. What is a Witch but someone that is guided by the wild rhythm of the Divine?** I was desperate to merge with an energy that I believed would give me freedom and solace, but it was something that I felt I had to find far and wide outside of myself. What I didn't see was that my own wild nature, the Wild Witch within, was in my shadow, so I kept projecting it outwards. Finally, at that moment, hysterical and lost in the woods with my dog amongst the moose, I realized the wild outside was not what I was seeking. What I was truly seeking was to access my own wild nature within.

The Divine Feminine is the wild that we seek.

Journal Prompts:

- What does this story rouse in you? Do you resonate with this story? What about it speaks to you?
- What about yourself do you see in my story?

The Undomesticated Witch

And here is the audaciously wild truth; The Divine Feminine is the Wild that we seek. For so many years I was desperate to find the wild in nature, in the exotic expanse of what this incredible planet could offer me. **But what my soul needed was for me to truly explore my inner nature. I was so concerned with the outer nature, that I thought I had lost the wildness of my own soul. Now, I understand it was never lost, only forgotten.**

For years I had meditated, read all the eastern classics, explored yoga, and worked to calm and control my mind. I believed that was the way to "freedom." This was what the mainstream spiritual and new age realm had taught me was going within. **Yet what I was fundamentally missing inside of this was being in tune and awake to the divine intelligence; that source of energy that pulsated through every living thing in the universe. I craved to know this power and source, intimately. Simply meditating to "calm my mind" so that I could be present was definitely helpful but it did not fill the deep unfulfilled hunger inside of me that wanted to merge with this force.** I wanted to commune with this energy, to feel it in my heart. I wanted to live a more sacred life, but I had no

109

idea what that looked like. I wanted to pray and feel this power inside of me and outside of me, but I didn't know how.

I did not know what that looked like because every text I had ever read that gave me guidelines for living a more sacred life was based in a kind of religion–led and ultimately guided by a male energy or God. Nowhere in that did I see myself, or feel able to fully exercise my power amidst that. Wicca, the only option that was more feminine-based, still felt hollow to me as well, with too much emphasis placed on manipulating reality through spells and chants. I didn't know what exactly I was looking for, all I knew was what didn't feel right inside of me. Learning how to meditate offered me a great reprieve from my overly active and mostly critical and fearful mind but it didn't even touch the wildness I was looking for. These were all spiritual disciplines that were guided by men and were still showing me that the way out of my current reality was by taming the wild and crazy thoughts within.

Now I can see clearly that invoking the sacred, paves the way to living a life of magic. When you begin to commune with this mysterious force on your own terms, without a book written by someone telling you how it should come through but instead using yourself as your own authority- communing with this energy as part of yourself, you begin to reactivate the wild within. As you begin to open yourself up to this force- this powerful, mystical, and potent force, you begin to see the magic embedded behind the material. You begin to feel the spirit behind the matter. This spirit, this force, is the Divine Feminine and it is ready to be seen and felt for what it is, inside, and outside of ourselves.

David Kowalweski put it so well in his book, *Deep Power: The Political Ecology of Wilderness and Civilization* when he said,

"Domestication is forcing a natural creature to stay somewhere it does not want to and preventing it from going somewhere it does. Domestication is therefore, immobilization of natural flow. It is the frustration of the heart's desire to go where it is pulled.[3]" What are we but wild Witches that have been taught and conditioned to mistrust our intuition? And what is intuition but Divine Intelligence working through us? Our wildness IS our deep feeling, is our gut, is this natural *flow* that Kowalweski talks about. The wildness IS the mystery, it is the wild wind, it is the wild ocean, it is the wild sky. It is our wild heart, our passion, our purpose. It is the sacred sight, it is being in tune with the energy of this planet and universe. The natural flow that Kowaleski talks about IS the sacred essence of the divine. It pulls us without us having any true understanding of how it works. It knows without knowing how it knows. This flow works through us, as us. It guides us slowly, it infuses our senses, it helps us return to our natural animal-like sensations. What is so beautiful about animals is that because they do not have a rationalizing faculty, they are at one with this flow. That, in essence, is wildness at its most pure. The animal when untouched by human doing, allows itself to be pulled by something greater than itself. That is the purest essence of being wild.

So what does this mean for us beings just starting to take our Witchy selves out of the closet? The crux of rewilding ourselves is allowing ourselves to re-sync up with this flow. This flow is ultimately based in our feeling. Our feeling is our deepest truth, it's how our intuition guides us. It is no wonder why so many of us have been so lost for so long. We have been trained out of our truth, our intuition domesticated, dismissed, and taught it wasn't worth anything. This is a silent and subtle energetic domestication that the divine feminine has endured for thousands of years. Women and some men were hung, burned, tortured, and beaten if they allowed themselves to be guided by this enigmatic and uncertain force. This force has no rules, this force has no laws. The one and only guiding principle of this force is that it is based wholly and fundamentally in the energy of Love. Does that mean that we understand it all of the time? No. Does that mean we can rationally argue its pull? No. Does it mean that we feel aligned with our feelings and actions, Yes. Does that give us a deep sense of inner power and strength? Yes. Does that take away all other outer authority? **Yes. Rewilding, the most revolutionary act any Witch can ever do.** This is the step of truly taking ourselves out of the closet, and allowing ourselves to be guided by this wild, pure, and powerful force. We become our own authority.

The human condition that our historical consciousness has exposed us to, has shaped, stifled, and all but eliminated our "natural flow." To be fully in tune with the natural flow would mean that one was aligned with no outer authority. For a woman to reclaim her own personal and ineffable connection to the divine as her own source, and ultimately her own authority, is to truly rewilding the self.

Journal Prompts:

- Where in your life have you stopped yourself from going where you feel naturally pulled?
- Where and when do you still do it?

Resonance

So now that we are able to understand what true wildness is, how may we begin to fully tap and open ourselves up to it? The answer is in one word, resonance. There are many definitions of resonance, as it is a scientific term just as it is an everyday layman's term. The mechanical definition for resonance is, "The condition in which an object or system is subjected to an oscillating force having a frequency close to its own natural frequency." And this is how we begin to allow ourselves to sync up with our own naturally wild flow.

Resonance isn't something that is thought or rationalized. Resonance is something that is felt. What does this verb, "to resonate'" really mean? It means that whatever you are exposed to, be it a book, a television series, a person, a place, a thing, anything, it means that you begin to pay attention to how you *feel* when you are exposed to these things. Resonance is based in vibration, it is how we vibrate with something. I love this quote by Rumi, "Allow yourself to be silently drawn by the strange pull of what you truly desire and it will not lead you astray." That strange, mystical, and not completely understood pull by any rational notion IS resonance.

Resonance is following our feelings, it is allowing ourselves to react instinctively to something. Do you have a favorite song? A favorite movie? A favorite person? You can easily name the reasons why you love something, but in its deeper more fundamental essence, there is easily something that cannot be named, it is simply a feeling. Resonance is based on that feeling and it acknowledges that there is a vibration in something that matches your own vibration, so that in turn you vibrate on a similar wavelength.

Everyone has their celebrities they resonate with. I remember when the show *Broad City* came out, it was like a part of me was on that show with those ladies. Abbi and Ilana were on my exact wavelength- on the edge of a kind of new feminine consciousness. The jokes they told were jokes I had made with my friends and family. The weird outlandish political statements they made were ones I had thought about over and over in my own head. I remember in their 4th season, they came out with an episode called, "Witches." It was right on the edge of the birth of this book. Gah-daym do I resonate with those ladies. It's hard to put into words what it is exactly except I vibrate on much of the same wavelength that they do, on the same consciousness tip. And that is what those women did- they gave voice to an emerging feminine revolution, the same way I am speaking to it right now.

Another person I have resonated with my entire life was Georgia O'Keefe. I love to make art, but the thing I seem to create over and over since I was a kid are flowers. As the flowers grew, so did the scale and beauty. My favorite thing to draw, and still to draw, are these giant, beautiful, vaginal flowers. I love to make their petals overflowing and the center of it this powerful evolving, orgasmic void. When I was exposed to Georgia O'Keefe, something in me resonated deeply with her work. I felt her vibe, and I expressed the same sentiment in my own artwork. It was the work of the feminine- of the deep, internal, beautiful, and mystical artistry of the portal through which all life emerges. What is more beautiful than that?

Let's bring up the obvious here, since I know some part of you resonates with this too; The Witch. I was a Witch almost every consecutive year from ages 7-17 for Halloween. To me, there wasn't really anything else to be. Any movie about Witches, any book that had Witches and magic in it...THAT. WAS. MY. SHIT. Funnily enough, I never became Wiccan, there was something there that I didn't resonate with. But the badass female who had magical powers? 100%.

Resonance. Begin to ask yourself, what is that I really resonate with? What kinds of people? What kinds of art? Allow yourself to become silently pulled, through resonance. Resonance is based on a feeling, it's based on an identification. Somewhere in something, you see and feel yourself in it. You feel pulled toward it. As the Divine Feminine emerges, and more of us women begin to follow our gut, find our power, and reclaim the Witch energy we lost so many years ago, more and more we will see ourselves in things, resonating.

Another way resonance can work for you is to begin to pay attention to what you do NOT resonate with. For instance, I do NOT resonate with the Kardashians. A few years ago, I finally looked up who the hell Kim Kardashian was. I couldn't figure out why the hell this woman was so famous? Was she a writer? An actress? Had she made some incredible work of art? No. She was good looking. And very rich. I was curious about why the hell she was so worshiped in our culture, she must be funny or deep or have something incredibly unique she is offering our planet, so I watched an episode of *The Kardashians*. I was confused because all I absorbed was incredibly vapid and empty gossip, discussions about looks and image, and an overwhelming obsession with fame. I was grossed out. That feeling was kind of repulsion...I wasn't silently vibrating at the same level, if anything my body was like, "Run in the other direction, now!" I definitely don't resonate with the Kardashians.

What I am doing here by naming resonance is shining a light on the things that have been glossed over and held underground for too long. Resonance is how the Everyday Witch navigates her material reality. It is syncing up with the wild divine, allowing your own internal rhythm to sync with those things that match your own. It's opening up to the pull of that resonance and paying attention to what you feel drawn to.

I challenge you to pick a day or chunk of hours living solely through resonance. Use the time to pay attention to what pulls you, what feeds you, what you feel energetically aligned with, and what you don't. The thing about resonance is that it can surprise us. And it also can begin to make our life very inconvenient. Because as we begin to be truthful with ourselves about what we feel and vibrate with, it may not fit into the constructed life that we have created. **Resonance isn't rational, which in a world based on reason means that it can create chaos and havoc. Yet it is this pull, this vibratory matching that will not lead you astray. It is this pull that is the deepest truth of yourself. And when we are aligned with our truth, we are in our highest level of integrity and self worth.**

Journal Prompts:

- Pick a "day of resonance" and journal about what happens, what are you drawn to? What repels you? Be as deeply honest as you can be, get to the bottom of your cup of truth, the wild + free space within.

Integrity

Integrity is not something that is typically taught to women. I feel like integrity is almost something that has been adopted as a masculine trait, that men have had more access too than women. This I believe is because things with integrity have an innate strength to them. It's like they are tied to something deeper in themselves, tethered to a kind of truth. There are a few different definitions for integrity on Google's dictionary, one is "The condition of being unified, unimpaired, or sound in construction." This definition lends itself a myriad of synonyms along the lines of strength, robustness, and sturdiness. This is why integrity has been aligned more with the masculine than the feminine up until now. It's been identified as a kind of strength, and classically, women were not taught to adopt such things. As in a patriarchy, it has been the burden of men to carry the weight as the father figure and the "voice of reason." Women were classically in the same category as the children, still needing a man to give them permission and allowance for their power.

Integrity was never something that was taught to me, it was only modeled as best it could be by my mother and occasionally my father. But no one ever directly talked to me about integrity, what it meant or how I could begin to adopt it as a part of my life.

My favorite definition of integrity is, "The state of being whole and undivided." This to me, is what true integrity means. So many of us have been walking this earth trained, our spirits domesticated by a kind of left-brained, patriarchal, rational energy. This energy pushes us dis-identify with our own internal compass, that which is our wildness and connection to the mystery. It's a dis-identification with our own wild feminine of everyone's wild feminine. So many people are walking around feeling depressed, lethargic, bored, and exhausted. I've seen client after client in my office that just feels empty. There is no other way to describe it, but a lingering emptiness that never seems to recede. They don't know what is

117

missing, all they know is that they are exhausted and depleted, usually kind of sick with something, and perpetuating a system that they can't find their own truth inside of.

The emptiness is the lack of Spirit. It's living one's life as a machine, basing all of one's decisions on what one *should* do, what seems *reasonable* and *smart*. It's using all of one's energy and life force inside of the mind, inside of the brain. What that does is discontinue the feminine, the flow, the spirit, and the mystery. It completely eliminates the pull of what truly feeds us by training and domesticating us to believe that we are fed by the rational and the rational only. This disembodies us, where we only engage with our brains, instead of our hearts and gut. It's separating the emotion from life experience and the feeling of something. It's cutting us off from the full spectrum of consciousness that is available to us as humans.

To live life fully embodying one's integrity means that your spirit and your mind are acting in unison and that they are in alignment. It was Gandhi that said, "Happiness is when what you think, what you say, and what you do are in harmony." This is close to that undivided state of integrity I am talking about except what I would add here is, "What you feel."

This is a hidden kind of integrity, the kind that we don't fully value or see as important within our culture. The monetary, financial, and appearance based values of the US have forced us to push aside the deeper more hidden kinds of integrity, the kind that only we ourselves know if we are operating inside of. How many of us worship someone who makes six figures and has all the material comforts? We see that person as the epitome of success and abundance. Yet, what is going on behind closed doors with that person...the pain they feel, their own inner struggle to endure inside of a job they feel empty within yet not dare to admit that to anyone, much less themselves, is where our true integrity resides. **Let's reframe what integrity really means; someone that honors the truth of their own soul and guides their life and actions in accordance with this truth.**

I want to dispel a myth here. For too many eons in our culture we had the belief that to be in alignment with what one feels and with what one does was an "impossibility" it was "just a dream", or "irresponsible". How many of us have been schooled and asked repeatedly by our parents and teachers, "Is that going to put food on the table?" If it was something we were passionate about such as art, music, or something that we felt aligned with on a visceral level, it was deemed "just a dream". Unless of course, you were blessed to come from a family that valued the power of art. This is all part of a rhetoric that belongs to an outdated and imbalanced patriarchal world order. This is an order that has perpetually dismissed the realm of intuition, feeling, and the deeper divine intelligence that is guiding us along. In a world where magic doesn't exist, and one is beholden to all life within a rational and mechanistic box, those statements ring true. What I am here to say is, "Not No Mo."

As we enter the age of the Divine Feminine and begin to live in our highest integrity, aligning our feelings with our actions and TRUSTING in this force, we will inevitably be guided to a life in abundance. What keeps so many people from aligning these two forces and living in their integrity is they have that nagging voice in their head that they will be poor and constantly struggling to survive. When one's dominant mode of thinking is based in the rational, of course, one would feel fear. The rational likes to have things under control, "to know," and to understand where one is going. If we don't have that foothold, we feel insecure and because of our conditioning, we feel a deep "mistrust." This is because we have never been led to believe in a deeper guiding force beneath all of this matter that is opening the way for us. Because of our intense distrust, our "fear" we look for proof of that mistrust everywhere.

This is where the rhetoric of, "we create our reality" rings just a little true. Wherever our consciousness is at any certain point is what we will see reflected outside of ourselves. What we are doing here with this work, is actively recalibrating the feminine within, shedding light on it, and most importantly beginning to TRUST in it. If we do not trust in this force, we can never give it a chance to show up for us in our lives. Because we have lived in a culture that has never seen this force as anything real, worthy, or valid there is no way that it could ever give this force credit or begin to trust it.

This perpetual myth of masculinity is what has kept us asleep to ourselves for way too long. It is the deep-seated fear that has kept us domesticated, living lives that are not true to us and working in careers that are not authentic to our own voice. When we are not living a life in alignment, it is very hard to embrace living a life fully in our integrity, no matter how good of a person we are. We live in a new era now, an era in which 50% of Americans are self-employed. As much as the internet and technology have enslaved us, they have also liberated us as it is now that we are emerging from large institutional structures that govern our entire lives and into more individualized business models, tailored for a certain clientele that is able to express whatever particular gift and energy it is that you are meant to offer the world.

It is time that we begin to take responsibility for our consciousness, meaning taking ownership of where we put our focus and attention. **As we begin to honor and venerate the mystery and unseen, and we begin to take the energies of the divine feminine out of the closet, we also honor that our own energy is part of the greater whole, and it is our own responsibility to begin to notice the things in the world that are changing for the good.** The old school institutionalized powers have kept their ruling order through fear, control, and rationality. We have been seeped in this energy for way too long. And now with the advent of 24 hour news and internet information we can get whatever information we WANT to see, at any time. This is where we begin to ask ourselves, what is it that I want to feed my consciousness? Is a fear induced PWC this the kind of world that I want to be a part of creating? Paying attention to where we place our attention, and looking for proof of that will begin to recalibrate your system towards the divine feminine.

Journal Prompts:

- Are you living a life in your integrity?
- Does your internal truth match your external actions? Where might you need some course correction?

WITCHY BITCH WISDOM

- Underneath all the reasoning and logistics we KNOW what to do, but because the culture doesn't honor intuition, we go with the rational, reasoned, and analyzed approach. Our culture directly trains us OUT of our intuition. It teaches us to not trust what we feel, and therefore we don't trust what we feel. We don't trust ourselves.

- This voice, this feeling that we have been trained out of feeling IS our wildness. The wildness is the natural flow-state. And it is the thing that we are so desperate to reclaim. It is the natural part of ourselves, the piece that IS Spirit.
- As you begin to open yourself up to this force - this powerful, mystical, and potent force, you begin to see the magic embedded behind the material. You begin to feel the Spirit behind the matter. This spirit, this force, is the Divine Feminine.
- The crux of rewilding ourselves is allowing ourselves to resync up with this natural flow-state. This flow is ultimately based in our feeling. Our feeling is our deepest truth, it's how our intuition guides us.
- Resonance is following our feelings; it is allowing ourselves to react instinctively to something. Resonance acknowledges that there is a vibration in something that matches your own vibration.
- Resonance is how the Everyday Witch navigates her material reality. It is syncing up with the wild divine, allowing your own internal rhythm to sync with those things that match your own. It's opening up to the pull of that resonance and paying attention to that which you feel drawn.
- To live life fully embodying one's integrity means that your spirit and your mind are acting in unison and that they are in alignment.
- As we enter the age of the Divine Feminine and begin to live in our highest integrity, aligning our feelings with our actions and TRUSTING in this force, we will inevitably be guided to a life in abundance.

Endnotes

1. Audrey Lorde, *The Masters Tools Will Never Dismantle the Masters House* (UK: Penguin, 2018)

2. "Everybody is a Genius. But If You Judge a Fish by Its Ability to Climb a Tree, It Will Live Its Whole Life Believing that It is Stupid." Quote Investigator, last modified April 6, 2013, https://quoteinvestigator.com/2013/04/06/fish-climb/

3. David Kowaleski, *Deep Power: The Political Ecology of Wilderness and Civilization* (New York: Nova Science Publishing, 2000)

5

Divine Receptivity: The Key to Embodied Self-Worth

"When you take a flower in your hand and really look at it, it's your world for the moment." -Georgia O'Keefe

Receiving. Ooooohweeee does this word make you cringe? Let me say it again, this time more slowly. R E-C-E-I-V-I-N-G. There are very few women and empaths on this entire planet that don't feel some sort of uncomfortableness when contemplating this word and action. One of my clients told me that thinking about receiving made her want to throw up, and the reaction can really be that intense. Why the hell is this? Well, **as women in a distorted world culture that prizes masculine energy and all the attributes that are attached to it, to receive would mean that we were opening ourselves up to our worth in a world that doesn't value or see our value**. It would mean that we were feeling our power, a deep sense of ourselves, our place, and we're grounded in our integrity.

If you are like the many very empathic, intuitive, sensitive, and creative souls that embody the feminine- to receive in a world that you have never felt recognized by for your worth, is almost an impossibility. There are two kinds of worth that I am talking about here, there is what our mainstream culture deems "worthy" or "worth something," and then there is how we feel about ourselves; our own personal internal sense of worth. The thing is that these two are not mutually exclusive, in other words, they kind of work hand in hand.

We are taught from birth that in order to be *worthy* you must do something that the mainstream system deems *worthy of*. In the American PWC, that comes down to money and looks. Yes, there is justice, and goodness, and moral rightness and this is definitely worth something, but our advertising and media don't make money from that. So the shallow parts of ourselves are emphasized and like it or not, we are bombarded with images of nearly perfect human forms- especially from movies and television from the time we are very little. **Wealth and beauty are prized in our culture as the ultimate sense of worthiness within the American PWC**. No wonder I have spent my entire life feeling like I could never quite hit the mark!

Because the standards of worth are almost impossible to truly inhabit in the American PWC, not to mention based on incredibly banal, vapid, and soulless kind of energy, what ends up happening is that the beautiful, sacred, and sensitive Witches of the world feel outcasted, rejected, and ever so slowly but ever so deeply feel more and more outside of the world.

And this is it, this is the crux of it. **For the empathic Everyday Witches of this world, if one does not fit into this box of worthiness based on the material, we are domesticated to believe that we are not worthy. What is truly ironic about**

this is that we have the medicine that this shallow, overly-rational, and soulless world needs, we are the deep feelers and intuitives, we are the Witches that have the connection to the unseen energy; we are the keepers of the mystery. Yet no one has ever taught this to us, no one has ever shown us the way, and not one person has ever told us that our power is worth anything. In a world culture that burns women alive (still done today by the thousands) for having "powers." it's no goddamn wonder we have kept our mouths shut, our eyes down, and internalized (maybe not consciously) every bit of bullshit they have thrown at us. It was the only way we were able to survive. What I am here to say today is Not No Mo'.

Agreeing with the status quo– even subconsciously has taught us to hide. Hiding has been what has kept Witches safe for millennia upon millennia. **What has happened to the world that is devoid of feminine intuitive power? It destroys, fights, and incites a kind of greed that has no bare end.** We are at a breakdown/breakthrough point y'all, and I'm telling you, it is up to us hidden, powerful, and intuitive Witches to shift the shit out of this paradigm. This begins with us getting really real about how we feel about ourselves, and what we believe we are worthy of, beyond what this sick society tells us we *should be*.

Journal Questions:

- Where in your life have you hidden or compromised your intuitive gifts to fit in? How, why, and where?
- What do you think would happen if you came out of the closet?

Worth and Receptivity

Because our worth is not something that can be measured or seen, only felt, it is only something that we ourselves will ever really know. It is also the only thing that we ourselves can give to ourselves. When we have a deeper sense of unworthiness and enter into a relationship with someone, what we are doing is feeling the energy of love from them which is beautiful and essentially what makes life worth living. The problem arises when we become attached to that love as a condition, in order to *be* a certain way and to *do* certain things in order to attain that love. This is the model in which we gain our sense of self-worth through their approval/love versus our own deeper integrity. This is conditional love. That is why so many of us need someone, or why we feel this deep emptiness inside that doesn't seem to go away. It's worth, and even deeper, worth is really a sense of love for oneself. When we enter into relationships without beginning to open to our own sense of personal self-worth, we will forever be enslaved to the other person and their image of ourselves through their eyes. We will need them in order to feel worthy and will go to great lengths to feel that love because without it we are left with our own empty sense of ourselves if we never cultivate it on our own.

I write this because I was this, and I know this. To me, there almost always has seemed to be a direct correlation between those that are extremely empathic, psychic, and intuitive and the lack of true self-worth because we have never been taught that our natural energetic gifts are worth anything or are a *real* power. All of our true power has been dismissed, and disintegrated, gone unseen, and therefore has gone to the dark places.

For me, because I was always such an outsider to this culture, being a Witch that never knew of her power or worth and never finding herself or her image anywhere reflected back to her in popular culture; I had no mirror and no validation from the outside world that gave me that sense of self-worth that others feel. Despite being a beautiful ½ Italian woman who was born gifted with sight, communication, and charisma, the only thing I was ever aware of was my gross ineptitude at fitting in. By around the age of 6 I started really hooking into the mass-connected consciousness and the weird shit people would judge each other on. I was so fucking sensitive, sensitive to everyone and everything, I was overwhelmed all of the time by the sadness and the pain, and so I ate to feel better. The food filled the void, and it also gave me love. I was lonely from a young age. I never felt included, I never felt like anyone else, and I always felt ugly. This perpetuated a deep level of unworthiness as the culture at large just served back to me what I was already ingesting from it, the blaring neon lights that seemed to reflect back to me wherever I went that read, "You Are Not Enough." Place a beauty queen mom with her own deep levels of shame and unworthiness masked in a constant need to lose weight and a chubby Italian father in the record business that was constantly snorting coke to get thinner, and you got a really exciting cocktail of Southern California dysfunction that was my life.

The thing I realize now so clearly is this deeply embedded sense and reflection of unworthiness was the direct barometer of how easily I was able to love myself. **In the new age spiritual world there is so much talk about learning how to love oneself and believe me, I have prayed, bargained, and given my entire being to Spirit to open myself up to this. What I found was that the answer was in the opening to receive, not forcing**

myself to create something. And this is how I want to begin to shift the narrative on self-love, from one of pushing and striving to instead of opening and allowing. As this is what truly opening to one's feminine power is about and centered in.

What if all we had to learn how to do was open to receive what was all already there waiting for us? THIS is what true receptivity is about, and it is how our true worth and sense of self will come through. It is not a matter of forcing and pushing to make something happen, because inherently when we are striving for a deeper change, we are coming from a place that something is innately wrong. And this is a very fine line to ride, as it is our human nature to want to improve, make better, and push to change. But because we have lost the art of believing in something deeper that holds and protects us, our ego has gotten way out of control inciting a kind of arrogance that dismisses the spirit behind the matter. Shifting one's focus to allowing versus pushing is simply a matter of opening ourselves up to what is already there, waiting ever so patiently to join forces with us. It is Spirit waiting to be acknowledged, seen, and divinely opened to. This is the introduction of an entirely new way of looking at reality.

Journal Prompts

- Where in your own life have you struggled with your own sense of worth?
- What does self-worth mean to you?

You Can't Run Away from Yourself

While I was in the midst of writing this book, I kept getting more and more signs from Spirit that it was time to move. Moving for me used to be my way of dealing with any kind of stress in my life. It's what was taught to me by my mom from a very young age. Growing up with a single mother doing her best to thrive and who did not live by ANY conventional standards, when any kind of shit hit the fan in our family, you better start packing up, cause we were moving. Have you ever seen the movie *Mermaids* with Cher and Winona Ryder? My life was kind of like that, except not in the 50's but in the 90's. My mom was literally beauty queen beautiful, free, and in her sexual power. She didn't operate by any normal American standard and was on her own internal hunt for the perfect life, wherever that may be.

Suffice to say, I absorbed this way of being throughout my life and oftentimes would live in 3 different places in a year. By the time I had ended up in Seattle though in 2015, my life was at a complete breakdown and I had hit my max for the number of times I had moved in a year. I counted 9 times that I had moved that year, that's right 9. You can always tell how my mental state is with how many times I've moved, obviously that year I had lost my shit.

Moving had always represented the best parts of a fresh start, new surroundings, and a new environment. A new me. The shadow side of that newness was always a dark space inside of me, where I was running, running, running away from all the shit that kept following me. These were things I had been running from my entire life, things that I felt I could overcome if I just changed locations. I ran for years and years, hoping to evade the pain that kept following me. These were deep emotional wounds with which I hadn't yet developed the right tools to cope. I felt deep levels of inadequacy and unworthiness, uncertain of how I would support myself or even thrive in a world in which I felt like a freak. I had done all of the things that one is supposed to do to "achieve." I spoke Arabic fluently, had been in the Peace Corps, knew how to organic farm, had become an herbalist, healer, and massage therapist, and had a graduate degree in Sustainable Communities something that I felt very passionate about. Yet there I was, age 32, and lost once again. All of my *achievements* simply a stack of papers, with a hollow inside still uncertain of the truth of my own soul.

Unbeknownst to me, I had landed in the perfect spot to dig into myself- Seattle, Washington where it rains 10 months out of the year and there is a palpable darkness. There is a lot of time spent *inside* in Seattle, and finally, at this point in my life, I had become so literally exhausted from running and running away, that I was ready to go inside, deep down in a way that I never had. I had spent my life striving and pushing and it had literally pushed me round and round in circles. I didn't have it in me anymore to keep pushing because what I was ultimately doing was running away from myself. My body and soul had been taken over by the masculine energy of *doing*. The feminine energy inside of me, my own intuition, and connection to spirit were weak and all but diminished. I was desperate for the feminine, not just because I needed to rest, but because I needed to trust in something bigger than myself, something that could make the decisions for me. I needed something that I could rely on, something that allowed me to let go, something deeper. All of that running made it clear as day that I didn't have any base or grounding. I didn't have anything that I could tether to, I was missing the deeper belief in Divine Intelligence. Of course, I had an altar and prayed. But there are layers and there are depths to this connection, and one can only truly begin to swim in its depths when one begins to fundamentally believe that this force has your back.

I was always the one in my family that was just kind of scraping by for survival. I had taken pride in this, as a creative and a rebel I didn't really want anything to do with the system. Having too much money for whatever reason represented a kind of selling out that I guarded myself against. I'm sure some of you reading this have identified with this archetype. It's the struggling artist/writer/creative that chooses their art and original vision over complying with the system and the *man*. I held this identity for years, taking pride in not having much and living on very little. I even made myself feel superior for various reasons, believing that I was living a life in my integrity. Now, at 36, I can see that all of these years struggling and developing this identity was a defense mechanism for trying to maintain my autonomy within a mainstream culture that I had no place within. I had been living on the fringes of society for years and years. After graduate school, I had no idea what to do, how I was going to support myself, or where the hell I belonged. And there my ex Luke popped up, telling me he would take care of everything if I just came and gave us another chance. And so I did, stuffing all my intuitive voicing deep down because, on the flipside of all of that, I was scared shitless. I didn't think I was capable of living in this world as an adult. I had so much to offer, yet I had almost no worth. The gifts I naturally was able to give were there but they had never been seen as valuable or worth anything, and therefore, I didn't feel that way either. We are, of course, the gifts that we have to give this world.

And this is the story that has been repeated for eons and eons. It's the story of a woman uncertain of herself or how she will make it in a world not built for her acquiescing to her fear and feeling that a man can handle it better than her. This is embarrassing for me even to write or admit to myself and you all, but it's the truth. It's the shadow side of the strong woman archetype, it's the part of me I never wanted to admit to or even look at. I had spent so many years carving out my identity and self, amidst a patriarchal world culture that was devoid of mystery, spirit, and empathy that I had become just like that thing I was fighting against, unable to come to terms with my weaknesses and vulnerabilities because I was fighting, fighting, fighting simply to survive.

As I discussed earlier, it was only a matter of time before our relationship dissolved. I felt like a prisoner, of my own doing with no money and no power. Luke had control of everything, and I in turn became the weakest I had ever been in my life. I remember sitting at my altar and praying as deep as I could. I was on my hands and knees balling. I was in Alaska at the winter equinox and it was dark, cold, and lonely. I had no money, no sense of self-worth. I was at a very deep low. I asked spirit to please help me, I needed help. What was different this time versus the other times in my life I had asked for help was that this time I was so exhausted that I didn't even have it in me to hold onto an outcome, or to obsess over how my prayer would be received. Because I didn't grasp or hold on, because I didn't sit around and notice what *wasn't* happening, and because I was just so utterly exhausted to even care, my human rational self completely surrendered to any outcome and therefore I was completely open to receive. Within a few weeks, I had gotten a job as a massage therapist at a Chiropractor's office who paid very well. This was the first job doing healing work I had ever gotten as I never took the test to receive my official license yet in Alaska you could practice without one!

This was the job that started me on the journey I am on today, writing this book. For the first time in my life, I had found a position that I was not only good at, but incredible at. Within the first month of working there, people were booking my entire schedule up. The chiropractor's clients were telling him I gave them the best massage of their lives, and finally, for the first time, I allowed myself to recognize I was a healer and had a gift. A tension grew between the chiropractor and me as I remember one of his clients saying to him, "She got more cracks out of me than you." He didn't like that and a palpable tension grew between us.

Journal Prompts

- Where in your own life have you avoided facing your own darkness?
- What is it that you run away to? Do you still run away?

The Road to Embodied Self-Worth

After getting that job as a massage therapist and becoming the healer externally that I always naturally was internally, a new energy emerged from me. For the first time in my life, I was doing something that felt right to me. That meant that my internal emotional and spiritual truth was reflected in my external actions. To me, this is the absolute truest definition of integrity. And this is what true integration of all parts of the self is about. As our shadow is known as the *darker* parts, but the darkness isn't bad — it is simply unseen. When we start to give voice and witness to these parts, we are integrating the more hidden aspects of the self (our feminine, emotional, and intuitive side) with the seen aspects of the self (what we show others, and the world, how we present ourselves and the actions we undertake). When these two are unified, and integrated, meaning the internal is being expressed externally, we are in our integrity. This means we feel whole. But what it really gives us is a deep sense of power.

Darkness isn't bad — it is simply unseen.

From the time we are babies we are force-fed a diet of *shoulds* in order to be accepted by "society" (i.e a bunch of people afraid of the opinion of others guided by a dissolving white male colonial order). We are trained out of our truth, of what we feel to be right for us. We are trained out of that voice, that feeling, and our intuition which are part of the deeper energetics that governs this universe guiding and protecting us. We are taught by this masculine dominant system that this energy is in fact wrong. We are taught not to trust ourselves or our truth and we are taught the opinions of others, and what "society" deems *worthy* is what we should base our life choices and direction on. What this creates is a schism between what we feel and know inside ourselves is right, and when followed brings about our ultimate joy and fulfillment versus what will pay the bills earn *status* and make others happy (many times our parents, or our own internalized voice that was trained by them.)

I see this over and over in my practice, as this schism leads to an absolute split in the self. It is when the soul/spirit are disconnected with the brain/rationality. What ends up happening in this battle is that the brain (which is trained by a misshapen and distorted system that disregards the emotional and intuitive guidance) wins and again and again we are led away from our truth, what our soul truly wants, and what God is actually pushing us towards. So the majority of us end up in jobs that are soul-sucking, trained in fields that are *reliable*, *safe*, and *sensible* (when in fact they are part of a desensitized and inhumane system that is killing the earth and ourselves) ultimately living lives that are not our own to be lived. This is where the split happens, where our lives become a constant stream of *doing* for the approval of everyone else and the deeply embedded domestication of our intuitive wildness is put out and disregarded.

This is the true reason we have so many people on medication in our culture. When anyone is placed inside of a box, trapped, and living a life that they get no real joy or power out of, something begins to happen to the soul, it feels unseen, unheard, and worth nothing. This deep depression is the perpetual dismissal of our souls' truth and the intuitive guidance and feeling we get from the spirit world urging us in a direction that will ultimately fulfill us in a way we may never consciously know. These directions may not make sense but they are extraordinarily powerful and ultimately reveal our deepest truth and destiny.

Journal Prompts

- Are you living your life in your 'integrity'? Meaning does your internal state/emotions/truth match your external actions/reality? (Its ok if it's not, that's a tall order)
- If it's not, where might some shifts take place so that you could?

Abundance is Natural

We have been trained in the linear and dualistic patriarchal paradigm that sees everything through a scarcity/fear lens. The rational is based in a kind of control, and it is fundamentally based in what it is that we do not have. It takes heed of the blank spaces and counts those. It focuses on the lack, which emphasizes the competition, which emphasizes greed. It is a belief that there is only one kind of way to make it– and that is by clawing, striving, and pushing your way to the very top no matter who or what you have to destroy to get there. That is essentially what *business as usual* means in America and explains why we have a country with no embedded empathy. This is also what makes us thrifty, carefully counting our pennies with the deeper energy of fear/not-enoughness behind our wealth.

The new paradigm, the paradigm of the Divine Feminine–the era that we are in the midst of birthing together is an era based in abundance. It is a fundamentally flipped way within which to view reality. The feminine is collaborative, not competitive. It is based in the Divine Feminine, which is founded in the natural and complete abundance of this earth. Knowing in our depths that we are taken care of and that all of our own fundamental needs will always be met. Look out your window and allow yourself to witness the incredible bounty of this planet. It is teeming with life.

It took me years to understand the phrase, "Nature abhors a vacuum." What the hell did this mean? It means that if you make an empty space anywhere on earth, it will naturally become filled. This is the natural flow of this earth; one of true abundance. This is the spirit of abundance, and it is what our earth and all of life are founded on. We have been hypnotized at large to believe that we have to fight, compete, and claw for survival. It is what has been programmed into us from birth as it is the fear that the PWC has used to control us for eons. Opening ourselves up to the truth, that this earth and planet are based in an abundant and prosperous order is the beginning of us shifting our paradigm. **All of the embedded self-disgust, "not enoughness" and pain we have endured at the hands of the human PWC is based in this competitive scarcity model that is simply NOT. THE. TRUTH.** As we begin to flip our narrative and begin to see the world for what it is, we automatically begin to open ourselves up to receiving what is already here for us.

Flipping this worldview and choosing to believe in abundance versus scarcity is one of the most radical acts we can do on this planet. You might be reading this thinking, "Well my 'reality' is very scarce, I have barely enough to make rent and I don't know how I am going to pay my bills this month." And I am not for one second denying that reality, I see you, I feel you, and I honor you. Hell, I was there for years. What I am saying is that we have been trained since birth to believe certain things about money which on a deeper level, connects to what our deeper held fundamental belief about the universe actually is, and like it or not, in many ways it is connected to how *worthy* society has deemed us and therefore, how worthy we feel about ourselves. Beginning to flip the script on receptivity and abundance is like shifting your consciousness to begin to focus on what we already have. It's opening up to the truth; you are a naturally abundant and plentiful being, you are of this natural cosmic prosperous order. It is fundamentally based in gratitude. We are mimicking the feminine form, the blessed yoni herself that opens to receive. The earth has everything we could ever need, and we are blessed, protected, and guided towards its healing abundance.

Journal Prompts

- Where in your life might you still be operating from a scarcity mindset?
- How do you think that mindset shows up in your life?

Gratitude, Receiving, Opening, Allowing

All of us have heard the narrative on gratitude, we have heard Oprah talk about her gratitude journal and every new age person discuss the importance of this. And yes, gratitude is important...when it's truly felt. We have lived in a society that has trained us to think, rationalize, and control our reality through thinking. What this leads us to is making long lists of the things we are grateful for, going over them, and thinking thinking thinking about them. What I am asking you to do here, is to enter into a FEELING space with gratitude. It's different. When we feel grateful, our hearts open and we are truly able to receive grace in its purest form. Gratitude in its purest form is opening to receive love. It's something beautiful, something delicious, something sweet, something happy. When we rationally process gratitude, we are skimming the surface, and are not actually allowing the love to penetrate our souls, to enter into our bones, and ultimately to fundamentally alter us. Because when we truly begin to FEEL gratitude on a visceral and connected level, we are sending ourselves the message that we are worthy, and this is what will fundamentally change our entire being.

My entire life I have rationally understood the idea of being present and the importance of this. Until I linked it to receptivity and feeling, I never *truly* understood it. I would meditate for hours when I was younger, doing everything I could to witness myself. It was always from a place of striving and perfection, always trying to be better, to be different, I thought that alleviating my suffering was through this constant striving. The irony was that I was striving to be present. That's an oxymoron! How can one strive to be present? Striving is an action pushing forward motion, presence is nothing, it just is. There is no striving in presence.

Until I began to flip the script and begin to look at presence from the perspective of the divine feminine, then it was as if everything fell into place. **Now I am able to understand that presence is the ultimate act of receiving**. It is also the only true exit point out of linear time and the world of duality. When we are fully present with anything, we become "a part of" not "apart from". We become one with every single thing around us, and in that, we fundamentally become incredibly abundant. The same is true if you are in the middle of the forest, at one with every living thing, or in an office cubicle. Every single thing that surrounds us, whether natural or human-made comes from the earth, comes from divine intelligence, and therefore is alive. When we start to move through the world opening ourselves up to this animating factor of reality and allowing things to be alive no matter what they are, we automatically feel more in-tune and at-one than we ever could have before. We also feel less alone, isolated, and in our own bubble. And this is where we start really opening ourselves up to true abundance. Because as we become more present, we open ourselves up to the multitude of aliveness, beauty, art, nature, and power in all of that.

The Pain of Enduring Pleasure
Because the Divine Feminine has been so unseen, dismissed,

and demonized for so many eons, we Witches had no outlet for our powers. This world culture has been shaped by men and the energies of the masculine. It has positioned the empathic, feeling, intuitive guides into the roles they feel most aligned with, the roles they can use their empathic abilities most; that of the caretaker. Still, in the 21st century, more than half of the world's women are destined for this role, many taking pride in it, while others chomping at the bit, desperate for any way out. I, myself, a powerful ass Witch with obviously a helluva lot to say, felt most comfortable in the role of caretaker up until about my 30's. I thought about being a midwife or psychologist for years, roles that assist and heal. Neither of them felt right though because there was a repressed power inside of me for which I had yet to find the right outlet. I had incredible empathy, but I also carried with me, a profound strength. I carried within me both the masculine and the feminine, and I was always searching for the right role/identity/occupation that would fit. I was trying to find myself within the PWC, a system not designed to compute the powerful energies of the Divine Feminine. A system that has made no space for the Witch. Until now.

As I began to deepen my spiritual practice and find the right teachers that would help me discover my hidden power and voice, I began to realize what it meant to begin to live in a mostly receptive state versus a mostly active state. Opening to receive was one of the single most important realizations and shifts on this journey. Opening to receive after a lifetime of over-giving (what we as women are trained from birth to do) is like trying to open my dog's mouth for his arthritis meds, his jaw is locked tight and impossible to get through.

Over-giving. Does this word sound familiar to you? Because my god was it familiar to me. **In a patriarchal world culture,**

the worth of a woman was not based on her psychic healing powers or her ability to commune with the spiritual realms and offer guidance to the masses as it should have been. No, a woman's worth was based solely on what kind of a caretaker she was or how pleasing to the eye she could be. Let's break this down. Within this system, as a woman, you gained your sense of integrity and identity on how well you provided for others. In this system, if a woman were to receive anything at all, she would be seen as being a poor caretaker, and bad at her job, which would make her unworthy i.e worth nothing. I discussed this earlier in the book, but I want to really delve into this now so that we can fully understand this because this is very real ladies, and the source of an incredible amount of true unworthiness that we ourselves have never been able to name or understand.

There is an undercurrent collective psychic energy that women and empaths carry around with them, whether or not they consciously know it. Think about a vortex. It's a physics term for a spiraling gravitational energy that has its pull from the inside. The vortex spiral is in every energy on the planet, from plants, to the way birth works, to the way galaxies move, to the way a hurricane operates- a vortex is when a kind of energy pulls for so long and so hard it takes over. We women have been inside of our own vortex, that of the PWC. Over-giving has been the pull. It has been the way in which we have found ourselves, our identity. It's this deep primordial urge that we cannot resist; the more empathic and sensitive you are the more you feel it. Over-giving is us giving every bit of ourselves and asking for nothing in return. It's been the only power we have had inside of a system that we have been robbed of all our power.

Now, I understand this is not the role all women play or feel now, in the 21st century. But what I am speaking to is a deeper energy that we hold from our mother's mother's mother's mother's. It's the collective unconscious and it's hidden inside the hearts of women. **The only real way to turn this tide and shift the energy that has robbed women of their power and men of their emotions is for us to begin to feel worthy of receiving.** Even if you are a career woman or a badass bitch doin' her own thing, there may still be deep down inside of you a latent over-giver. Or you may have gotten over your need to over-give, but have absolutely no idea how to receive.

I mean, us badass bitches of the 21st century don't want to identify with this energy, but it's there, it's our shadow, and it's real. And the more we cozy up to it, see it, and open ourselves up to its truth, the easier it will be to transcend and move through it.

Starting to open yourself to receive after a lifetime of feeling unworthy of receiving is literally painful. The receiving feels so foreign and so unholy that it's just easier to push it away and give instead. Yet this is how the deep furnace of resentment builds inside of us- the pit of anger that nothing and no one can successfully quell. It's our own self-fulfilling destructive prophecy that only we can shift. And it starts by opening to receive, no matter how physically, psychically, or emotionally painful it is. The kind of receiving I am talking about here is not a superficial kind of receiving. It's not shallow, easy, or undisturbed. No. The kind of receiving I am talking about here is opening up to a feeling of receptivity, of allowing goodness in. This occurs in the heart and through the emotions. Women have been dependent on the love of a man for millennia in order to receive that kind of love, it's what this system has taught us is what we want and also what will make us more worthy. Opening to true abundance and self-worth on the deepest levels means that we begin to receive the bounty of this earth in the present moment. We take it in, breathe it in, and feel it in. We emote, we open, we allow the purity, beauty, and goodness to touch us. Because as we do that, we begin to see ourselves in that beauty and begin to realize that we ourselves are that beauty. We cannot love ourselves if we cannot love the earth or each other. What we begin to notice externally will translate internally.

Journal Prompts

You might have to meditate deeply on these questions, it might be hidden away.

- Where in your life is it the most difficult to receive?
- How do you feel when you receive?
- How do you feel when you give?

The Physicality of Receptivity

As I was writing this chapter, wondering whether or not it was finished and contemplating its flow, my fluffy and adorable Shitzu-Maltese, Nico, came and plopped himself down on my chest. He did not ASK for attention; he demanded it. And that is how it usually goes with our animals. At this point, he is just an extension of me and is completely in tune with my energy. I've been feeling a little off lately, and he knew it. Overthinking and over-contemplating, all of it. Nico put his furry face in mine and started licking me all over. I could feel myself as he did this, tensing up, wondering when he would be finished so I could work on my book. But it was exactly that, at that moment, that I realized I was being un-receptive to him, meaning I was keeping him OUT. The truth was, I needed those licks, and Nico knew it. The question was, could I open up to allow that goodness versus stressing about how good something was? And how could I not open to receive this animal, this pure goodness? After all, dog spelled backward is God. And sometimes, I feel closest to God when my dog is loving me, as it is just pure love with no in-between or rational thought.

And that is just it. Sometimes rational thoughts keep us from opening up to receive the moment through being and our emotions. I noticed my body thinking about my next move in this book; it was tense. I could literally feel all throughout my body this holding-on feeling. Rationality helps us discern, but it often keeps us in a loop of criticality and tension that has become our modus-operandi here in the west. We are so connected to the active principle of DOING and THINKING that our bodies and energetic BEING stay in this state of constant tension, needing to be on the mark and ready at any moment to respond or retaliate.

Journal Prompts

- When do you keep pleasure OUT, and when are you most UNreceptive?
- Does your pride ever get in the way of you truly receiving? If so, where?

Why Manifesting is Actually Madness

We can't talk about receptivity without discussing manifesting. And believe me, I had to learn the super hard way that following the *law of attraction* actually just led me down a path to true and utter madness. I say this because I became so *into* this way of living (that trains you to pick the thoughts you think carefully and begin to solidly believe them, so you *create* the life you want) that I became totally fearful of any thoughts I had that were *negative* and started blaming myself intensely for anything that seemed *bad* that occurred in my life. I also just started manifesting stuff that wasn't right, it was off somehow or someway and I didn't understand why until I began to live life in a more receptive way.

Manifesting is still built upon the idea that darkness, the shadow, negativity need to be avoided and trained out of us at all costs. It dissuades us from our truth because there is no human on this earth that doesn't feel pain, hardship, or go through some kind of emotional strife. It doesn't exist. **What the manifesting mindset trains us to do, is bypass our pain, pretend it doesn't exist, and stuff it under the carpet. It also sends us the message that we should not be having those emotions, which innately pushes us to dismiss our truth, our authentic voice, and ultimately, ourselves. So we push ourselves to become something else, something that isn't true to how we are feeling in that moment**.

There is a very fine line here that needs to get ridden, because yes, there is definitely truth to changing your thoughts will change your reality, I will not deny that. And there are so many of us out there, like myself who are vulnerable and in need of a change. Manifesting can seem to give the person more control and power over their lives, and their thoughts. I believe that shifting our focus to look at the positives in our life is an important aspect of receptivity, yet, when this behavior becomes toxic is when we go so far as to deny the truth of whatever emotion we are having.

I believe that practicing manifesting in this way is actually a kind of black magic because what we are doing is putting our human will onto the divine flow. The basis of this book is based on the fundamental belief that there is a true loving and guiding force that is Divine Intelligence. This force is Love itself. It is the force that makes our hearts beat, makes birds fly, and makes stars shine. This book is a manual to sync up to that flow so that it can begin to work through you and for you, and that you become in tune enough with yourself, your intuition, and your emotions so you know when it is guiding you. That is being in a receptive and active state, working with this force. When we are working on manifesting without having really aligned with this force, what we are doing is using our human will which is mostly reacting from a very human "race consciousness" and status quo (which is sick and distorted) kind of mentality to affect our reality. There is nothing wrong with having human wants, but if we are pure willpower without having the grounded connection to spirit, we are simply feeding our egos which doesn't give us the ultimate satisfaction and true, authentic power that we desire. **Authentic power is when we align with this flow and use ourselves as a conduit to serve it. As we begin to serve it, it will automatically provide for us. This is also the definition of integrity, when our internal state and truth match our external actions.**

It took me awhile to fully realize this. I so wanted to believe that if I tried hard enough to have a million dollars, I could have it, simply through my own willpower. So much of us just think if we had a little more money, our lives would be so much easier, right? The truth about this is that money is really just energy. And until we begin to address the deeper levels of our own worthiness, it will be difficult for us to attract material worth, i.e money. I especially believe that this is true for old souls, like yourself reading this book. We have come here to learn cosmic lessons, and oftentimes those lessons force us to confront the deeper spiritual aspects behind all the matter around us, all the stuff, toys, and physical cash.

I remember when I was super into the *law of attraction* work, I was kind of at a major low. I didn't have the tools to access these deeper teachings yet and was desperate for something that relieved my pain. My dad had just died, I was out of shape, I had just left my boyfriend, and I had virtually no money delivering food with my fancy master's degree education. I was so into this manifesting work, writing myself into a frenzy every morning and night– kind of hypnotizing myself into a more positive mindset and state. I didn't know what else to do. I think it was about the 20th of the month and rent was coming due. I needed $1,200 in 10 days and I think I had $40 in my bank account. Still, I believed I could manifest this money. I had no other choice!

One night while delivering food on one of those apps, I stopped my car to run and deliver someone's food behind another house. I was searching for the address and finally found it. On my way back, I was walking back to my car when all of a sudden out of nowhere a car backs directly into the side of my car. It was like the whole thing was in slow motion and as I saw the person backing into me, I ran to try and stop them, getting there way too late. When approaching my wrecked car, I noticed that I somehow parked in front of someone's driveway, something I don't think I have ever done in my entire life. In that literal 2 minute period, the man backed into my car. The passenger side back door was completely wrecked, and the side panel was totally messed up as well. Well, you can guess where this story is going. I find out that the insurance company estimated the damage at almost 3K, and instead of getting the car repaired, I decided to take the money so that I could pay my damn rent. The funny thing is, I think at the time I thought I was a manifesting badass. I didn't want to even face the reality that my sweet little Prius was fucked up. The money I was willing into materiality came to me, so great. I drove around with that dent in the side for 4 YEARS. It was literally a thorn in my side.

And this is a great example of what happens when we use the human will to get things that are not in alignment with the cosmic flow– accidents happen, and things turn out kind of awkward, weird, or out of sync. I have so many stories like this from my manifesting days, where nothing materialized, or what did materialize was a distorted, weird version of what I wanted. This kind of "creating without connecting" as I like to call it is devoid of the spirit, the connectedness, and the in-tune (intuition) that we use to guide ourselves along in this life. Much of the manifesting mindset as it stands is missing the sacred; it is focused on the human power and will to create, but without the depth and soul of truly connecting to Spirit. **When we ground ourselves in the Divine, we automatically become more receptive, we are attuned to a different frequency. We are in a state of opening and allowing versus simply creating and doing, which is what the manifesting world is based in. We begin to align ourselves with the sacred essence behind the object, with the spirit behind the matter, and in that, we feel a deeper connection to every-thing.**

If you engaged in any history class in America, somewhere over the years you were most likely introduced to the idea of "Manifest Destiny." As I can recall, this was a belief that

Americans had a God-given right and entitlement to manifest and create their own destiny and life. As I remember it being taught to me, this was a good thing. It promoted the power of this country to create itself in its own image, and to open itself up to its own man-made creative imagination. What I discovered about this phrase when doing a little digging, was that it was coined by president Polk (1845-1849) and what it did was give complete permission to all white men through the "word of God" to vanquish, harm, and kill all people of color, including Native Americans and African-Americans in order to "create" their ideal world. It perpetuated the idea that the white colonial order had been destined by God to take over the lands of North America and that the whiter you were the more *holy* you were. Well, that day is fucking over. What I'm here to say today is, Not No Mo' Bitches. The Divine Feminine is rising and this toxic patterning is dissolving as we submit to the higher empathic, feeling, and intuitive energies of this earth and its peoples.

Creating and manifesting is part of being human and it is a healthy expression of masculine energy but it must be balanced by knowing when and how to yield. It must be balanced by engaging with our hearts, our intuition, and with the energetic realm. That is what makes for true health, health of our souls, health of our bodies and communities, health of a nation, and health of mother Earth. We are a dis-eased culture because we have been so out of balance for so long. The Rise of the Divine Feminine is what is bringing the true empowerment to all this earth is so desperate for, and it comes with beginning to harness and fundamentally embody and understand the power of receptivity and yielding.

WITCHY BITCH WISDOM

- There seems to be a direct correlation between women and men that are extremely empathic, psychic, and intuitive and the lack of true self-worth because we have never been taught that our natural energetic gifts are worth anything or are a "real" power.
- Because we have lost the art of believing in something deeper that holds and protects us, our ego has gotten way out of control inciting a kind of arrogance that dismisses the spirit behind the matter.
- From the time we are babies, we are force-fed a diet of "shoulds" in order to be accepted by society. We are trained out of that voice, that feeling, and our intuition which are part of the energetics that govern this universe, guiding and protecting us.
- Together, we are in the midst of birthing the new paradigm of the Divine Feminine, an era based in abundance. The feminine is collaborative, not competitive, knowing in our depths that we are taken care of, and that all of our own fundamental needs will always be met
- When we feel grateful, our hearts open and we are truly able to receive grace in its purest form. When we rationally process gratitude, we are skimming the surface, and not actually allowing the love to penetrate our souls, to enter into our bones, and ultimately to fundamentally alter us.
- Starting to open yourself to receiving after a lifetime of feeling unworthy of receiving is literally painful. The receiving feels so foreign and so unholy that it's just easier to push it away and give instead. Yet this is how the deep furnace of resentment builds inside of us - the pit of anger

that nothing and no one can successfully quell. The kind
of receiving I am talking about is opening up to a feeling
of receptivity, of allowing goodness in. This occurs in the
heart and through the emotions.

· This book is based on the fundamental belief that there is
a true loving and guiding force that is Divine Intelligence.
This force is Love itself. This book is a manual to sync up
to that flow so that it can begin to work through you and
for you, and that you become in tune enough with yourself,
your intuition, and your emotions so you know when it is
guiding you; that is being in a receptive and active state,
working with this force.

6

Shedding Your Skin: Embodied Transformation for a New Era

"The Universe is Transformation, Life is Opinion." - Marcus Aurelius

Transform: To Change the Voltage of an Electric Current. This is my favorite definition of what it means to transform because it feels the most authentic. Many of us live our lives doing the same thing over and over like Groundhog Day or the Truman show. We keep with our same routines, our same thought patterns, our same choices. We feel this keeps us stable and safe. Change scares many of us as it provokes a feeling of being out of control, unable to "know" what is next. This fear of the unknown is what keeps us locked in our own self-imposed cages, our souls so very desperate to get out but bound by our own fear of the unknown. And because so many of us have not established a deeper connection to the Spirit world we cannot tolerate such changes, as our connection to the material and the rational is what keeps us feeling safe and secure. We numb ourselves, with medications, endless scrolling on our phones, and constant distraction to fill the void of spirit. We grow more and more empty, believing anyone and everyone in positions of "authority" to direct our life. We abandon our own internal autonomy and power because at the deepest level we fear ourselves and the consequences of what awakening this power would mean for our own lives.

Transform: To Change the Voltage of an Electric Current.

This is the pattern I have witnessed over and over in every single person that has come to see me for counsel, including myself. Humans are desperate for a deeper connection to their souls, the earth, and the cosmos but many have no idea how to get there. Here in this book, you have a guide to restoring that connection and reclaiming your true spiritual power. And if wholeheartedly committed to, this book will change your life. If every chapter is contemplated, exercised, and integrated into the self there is no turning back. A light gets illuminated within the soul that can never be extinguished. This is in fact what awakening is, "an act of waking from sleep." **So many of us have been asleep to our higher selves, and the divine within our own souls our entire life. Bringing light to this part of ourselves once seen and acknowledged changes us forever.**

And that is what the final week/chapter of this program embodies: Transformation and the birth of a new self. How many of us in our deepest most private moments wish to be someone else. The social media saturated culture of today has conditioned many of us towards our appearance. Many of us wish to be more beautiful, more talented, more of a star. But if you move past those ideas of what we feel we want, what we truly desire is simply to be SEEN. But we can never truly be seen if we do not allow ourselves to let go of the conditioning that has kept us in the dark all of our lives.

What is the Alchemy of Transformation?

The journey all of you have taken throughout this book has literally brought light to the darker and usually subconscious parts of our being. When something is in a subconscious place, it is in a place where we are not conscious of it, we simply REACT from it, but we have no power or control over it. What shadow work and this book/program have done is bring light to those darker places. When we bring light to a place that was previously not part of our conscious understanding, we EXPAND our field of consciousness. This is akin to the phrases illumination + awakening. What we are doing in this process is expanding the LIGHT of conscious awareness in our own selves which TRANSFORMS us. This is the alchemy of transformation as we are no longer operating from the same mode/size/kind of consciousness within which we were before. We have expanded, and therefore we have changed.

This process can be sticky sometimes because our families and friends get used to us being a certain way, hell, we get used to us being a certain way. It gives us stability to react and remain the *same.* But one cannot evolve if one is continuously stable. And evolution IS synonymous with transformation and the ability to let things "go" and allow ourselves to gracefully move on.

What it means to *Let Go*

Throughout this book, we have agreed that there is a cosmic flow moving through us and around us at all times and that the more we attune to this flow, the easier and smoother our lives become. To truly begin to live a new life as a DIFFERENT person and begin to embody the energies of transformation, we must fully release ourselves to this flow. There have never been 2 words that so completely describe the process of transformation than *let go*. And there have never been two words that have been harder for humanity to embody than *let go*. I'm sure I don't have to talk to you about this as every single one of us on this planet is ATTACHED to things. We have bonds that create identities, we have connections that create comfort. Yet the truth is that we are constantly evolving, constantly moving on this beautiful blue sphere around a giant ball of fire in this ever-changing space. Letting go is part of this process of change. Yet, so many of us deny this part of ourselves. We choose to stay the same because we are afraid of what may be on the other side. **The only way we can truly begin to move and flow with this cosmic energy that is constantly changing and shifting this universal current around is to begin to TRUST that it has our back, and ultimately our freedom embedded inside of it.**

Let's break this down for a minute, let's simply look at the word, "let." To Let: not prevent or forbid, allow. So another way of saying let would be, *to allow*. Now let's look at the word "go". Go: Leave, Depart. In essence, we are allowing something to depart. This entire book has been about aligning ourselves with the cosmic rhythm of this universe; the ever changing flow that moves along as a running river. It is what the Taoist called the Tao, The universal current/energy that moves, changes, and evolves. This current is ever running and is ever changing. If there is one thing we can count on is that it never remains the same. The only constant is change as the old adage says. All of this points to the POWER of this phrase, to LET GO, "Allow something to move." **This movement from holding tight to allowing something to move freely, moves us from control to receptivity. To be in a receptive state is to fully engage with the energy of this universe.** It is to allow yourself to constantly change, move, grow, and LET GO. To let go is to Let the universe GO as it is meant to, as its natural state is to move forward, shifting, moving, and dancing along. This is the crux of the human shadow. We all know too well what it is like to fear the unknown. We fear it for every reason imaginable, but at our core we fear it for our own security. So many of us, if we truly aligned ourselves with the flow and began to easily LET the universe GO as it pleases, we would be potentially facing a slew of consequences. The main one being our sense of identity, be it financial, tribal, or any other way your identity is held dear to you. Many of us feel that there is just too much at stake. There is a deep and rooted "identity" that we have created that is centered around our stability and security.

To let go is to Let the universe GO as it is meant to.

If we were able to shift our vantage point from the material to the spiritual, and begin to root ourselves and our entire existence in that truth, we would have such an easier time letting go. Because we wouldn't get as invested in the material as our ultimate truth. We would identify the spirit behind the matter FIRST as the energizer and creator of all things and with that realization begin to move and flow easier and with more freedom and ease.

Freedom

157

And isn't that the reason all of us are doing spiritual work? Aren't we all yearning somewhere deep inside of ourselves to be set free? Many of us yearn for freedom, but we don't even necessarily know what it is. We blame our partners, our jobs, our children, or any scenario in which we feel locked inside. We point the finger to everything and everyone around us except for ourselves. The truth is that real freedom is an inside job. We can grant people in positions of power authority over our own freedom, but then we are always privy to their judgment. To truly reclaim our own power, we must reown our own freedom and see it as the thing we give to ourselves. It is only when we feel imprisoned that we are. That is why a true and realized connection to a source that is outside of ourselves is the most important, as having a deep faith in something beyond our material surroundings, no matter how bleak, is what grants us this freedom. When we carry this connection to the mysterious, we are able to cultivate a faith that brings us our own inner sense of security and power that no person, place, or thing can take away from us. This trust in the unknown and the conviction with which this trust is cultivated is the foundation of freedom.

Plutonic Power

It is hard to talk about the process of transformation without talking about the archetype of Pluto. As an astrologer, Pluto is the deepest and most transformative area of any person's chart or life for that matter. It RULES the energy of death and rebirth, as well as some of the darkest parts of ourselves. It simultaneously rules complete and absolute liberation- as we shed those dark aspects of ourselves to become reborn. It can be a catalyst for absolute rebirth of the self. At its deepest though, Pluto is one with our deepest attachments to things and the process of releasing or "letting go" of them. At its core, Pluto is the highest POWER we can attain in this lifetime, once we are liberated from our attachments. And it is not having power OVER others, it is a mastery of the self. My favorite astrologer Steven Forrest talks about two archetypes of Pluto in his book *The Inner Sky*, represented in history, that of Adolf Hitler, and Gandhi. Both of these figures represent the deepest power of Pluto, both in completely opposite ways. Adolf Hitler was the lower vibration and dark side of Pluto, where he used obsession, control, manipulation, and murder to move energy on the planet. Gandhi, on the other hand, used empowerment, faith, vision, and the internal spiritual power. Both men moved entire nations, one through control, the other through freedom. But the deepest source of the plutonic energy lives inside of both of these men, and it begs the question: have you mastered your own fear? Because at its very core, Pluto represents one thing: Fear. Do we allow the fear to eat us alive? Always avoiding it, skirting from it, and hiding as best as we can from it? Or do we look at it- square in the face, transcend its power over us and allow ourselves to discover what is on the other side, freedom.

That is the process we have gone through in this book, looking at our own darkness square in the face and choosing not to run from it but instead allow ourselves to face it, and all of the pain that goes with it. Not running from our own pain is what actually brings to us the most power of anything. Because that is what the entire world is run on, it is what motivates most humans to hide themselves and their light: fear.

The moment we stop projecting our energy outwards, and start working to process, integrate, and control our OWN energy, we not only have more power than most of humanity, but we are free from the darkness of others.

Transformation

I'm here to let you all know that it is safe to let go. In fact, this is what the universe is begging of you to do. This is what makes us one with the powers that govern this universe, and it's what aligns us with our ultimate spiritual power as humans on this planet. The entirety of this book is to align with this hidden force that governs the universe and allow ourselves to be taken with it. This forces us to confront our control issues, our fear, and our sense of personal safety in order to surrender to something bigger; an authentic trust in a force much larger than ourselves. What the universe is asking of you is not just this theoretical "idea." It isn't just words on a page to skim over and contemplate when it's convenient. No. This is a true and authentic practice of shedding our skin. Leaving behind our ego identities to birth a new self. It is surrendering to the only one and true universal principal, renewal. I like to ask myself how many lives can I life in this lifetime? How much of my ego can I surrender in service to the greater cosmic current? Because it is this release of former ideas that limited us, and the embracing of the unknown that will bring to us our ultimate power. The reason this aligns us with our power is because this *unknown* place is based solely on a feeling. We cannot see what lies before us, but we can FEEL what is in alignment. And the more sensitive we become to what feels right rather than what looks right, the more powerful and in alignment with the flow we will become. This is to be able to walk by faith and not by sight and it is what every great spiritual being on this planet has learned to master. This is the key y'all, this is the secret.

So you need to get really real with yourself, this whole idea of trust, intuition, and accessing your shadow- is it just a theoretical concept you are implanting inside of your intellect?

160

Or is it something you TRULY believe in? Is it grounded inside of you? I have given you every tool inside of this book to access that flow and cement it into your reality. Sitting at your altar on the daily, praying, and acknowledging this energy is where you initiate the process. But the true faith and power comes to full fruition when we start aligning our actions with what we feel internally to be true. That means taking risks, moving outside of our comfort zone, and TRUSTING WHAT WE FEEL TO BE TRUE. This is the true gateway to power and absolute fulfillment of potential. Because that is all we are on this planet, vessels of potential. The potential cannot be actualized unless we employ and exercise our SPIRITUAL POWER meaning a deep and true acknowledgment of the hidden, unseen energies that govern this universe. We must work with them, integrate them into our daily lives, and above all else, FOLLOW ITS GUIDANCE. For then, we become one with this current, and our lives begin to flower like a rose during springtime.

So, I am here to ask you, and for you to ask yourself; Do you trust in this invisible force? Are you willing to start acting in accordance with its guidance? Because the answer to these two questions will determine whether you shed this skin you are sick and tired of and this identity as a victim of a system with no way out of. The answer to this will determine whether or not you begin to truly own your power. And become like the butterfly, free to do as she pleases and blowing right along with the wind. The butterfly is light as a feather, unhinged to the darkness moving freely throughout this beautiful ether. The choice is yours. I've given you the keys the question is whether to not you will unlock the door and discover the power and freedom that lies on the other side of this one and true precious existence.

Performative Ritual

- I'd like you to sit at your altar and bring in some symbolic objects that represent TRANSFORMATION for you. Is there a crystal that symbolizes this energy? A type of candle? Is there a tarot card? What energies are you releasing and what are you ready to bring in? I'd like you to meditate and get very clear on this for yourself as this will direct the flow of the ritual. Then I would like you to meditate on what kind of material objects you can bring in to support this releasing/rebirth process.
- Some objects I would consider including are: Sage + palo santo for the opening and closing of the ritual, a tarot card that represents the energies you are bringing in and/or releasing– one or both of these, a candle, and any object that has special meaning to you that symbolically represents whatever it is that you are bringing in/releasing.
- Open the ritual with your opening prayer and then clearly state your intention for this ritual. My intention for this ritual is to _____. At this point in my life, I am ready to let go/release _____ and I actively open to receive and embody the energies of _____.
- Burn the palo santo to initiate the energy, state your intentions and allow yourself to meditate on the burning away of what is inside of you and is dead/not aligned with your higher self/truth energy at this time. Imagine that part of yourself burning away. You can write down your intentions if you like on a piece of paper and burn it if you

like as a material representation of what is burning away inside of you.

- After that has burned away and you have imagined it releasing away from your body, bring in the energy you are focusing on and attuning to. Sit and meditate/vibrate with this energy. The more you can imagine this energy as a PART of you, you are accessing and enhancing versus something that is OUTSIDE of the self you are trying to attain, the quicker the connection/syncing. You are RELEASING and focusing something that is already inside of you that has been blocked up until now, we are actively releasing that block and then focusing on bringing forth that which is inside of you and wants to come out. This is very different than trying to manifest, this is the FEMININE way of allowing it to come forth, attuning to the flow, and accessing the truth that already resides within.
- Sit for as long as you need at your altar feeling this power. Close the ritual with some gratitude, and voila!

WITCHY BITCH WISDOM

- There is a cosmic flow moving through us and around us at all times and the more we attune to this flow, the easier and smoother our lives become. To truly begin to live a new life as a DIFFERENT person and begin to embody the energies of transformation, we must fully release ourselves to this flow.
- When we carry a connection to the mysterious, we are able to cultivate a faith that brings us our own inner sense of security and power that no person, place, or thing can take

away from us. This trust in the unknown and the conviction with which this trust is cultivated, is the foundation of freedom.

· The moment we stop projecting our energy outwards, and start working to process, integrate, and control our OWN energy, we not only have more power than most of humanity, but we are free from the darkness of others.

· The entirety of this book is to align with this hidden force that governs the universe and allow ourselves to flow with it. This forces us to confront our control issues, our fear, and our sense of personal safety in order to surrender to something bigger; an authentic trust in a force much larger than ourselves

Endnotes

1. Steven Forrest, *The Inner Sky (Borrego Springs: Seven Paws Press, 2012)*

Bibliography

Forrest, Steven. *The Inner Sky. Borrego Springs: Seven Paws Press,* 2012.

Jung, Carl. *The Earth Has a Soul: C.G Jung on Nature, Technology, and the Human Soul.* Berkeley: North Atlantic Books, 2002.

Kowaleski, David. *Deep Power: The Political Ecology of Wilderness and Civilization.* New York: Nova Science Publishing, 2000.

Lorde, Audrey. *The Masters Tools Will Never Dismantle the Masters House.* UK: Penguin, 2018.

Moorjani, Anita. *Dying to Be Me.* Carlsbad:: Hay House, 2022.

Pinkola-Estes, Clarissa. *Women Who Run with the Wolves: Myths and Stories of the Wild Woman Archetype.* New York: Random House, 1992.

Thomashauer,Regena. *Pussy.* Carlsbad: Hay House, 2018.

Turner, Toko-pa. *Belonging: Remembering Ourselves Home.* Vancouver: Her Own Room Press, 2018.

"Everybody is a Genius. But If You Judge a Fish by Its Ability to Climb a Tree, It Will Live Its Whole Life Believing that It is Stupid." Quote Investigator, last modified April 6, 2013, https://quoteinvestigator.com/2013/04/06/fish-climb/

About the Author

Chase was born a natural mystic and has spent the majority of her life in search of truth and freedom. This has taken her all over the world from serving in the Peace Corps Morocco for 2.5 years to living alone out in a cabin out in the woods of Alaska. She is wild, and her intention is to help rewild those that have forgotten their true nature. She has a private practice in Joshua Tree, CA.

You can connect with me on:
- 🌐 http://www.chasebuttice.com
- 🔗 https://www.instagram.com/chasebuttice

Subscribe to my newsletter:
- ✉ http://www.chasebuttice.com

Made in the USA
Columbia, SC
25 July 2024

39319729R00112